PAYING THE PRICE
Women and the Politics of International Economic Strategy

EDITED BY *Mariarosa Dalla Costa and Giovanna F. Dalla Costa*

ZED BOOKS
London and New Jersey

Paying the Price was originally published under the title
Donne e politiche del debito by FrancoAngeli,
Viale Monza 106, 20127 Milano, Italy, in 1993.
This English language edition was first published by
Zed Books Ltd, 7 Cynthia Street, London N1 9JF, UK, and
165 First Avenue, Atlantic Highlands, New Jersey 07716, USA,
in 1995.

Cover design by Andrew Corbett.
Laserset by Opus 43, Cumbria, UK.
Printed and Bound in the United Kingdom
by Biddles Ltd, Guildford and King's Lynn

A catalogue record for this book
is available from the British Library.

US CIP data is available from
the Library of Congress.

ISBN 1 85649 297 4 Hb
ISBN 1 85649 298 2 Pb

DEDICATED TO DARIO, IVO AND GIANNI

CONTENTS

ABOUT THE AUTHORS

C. GEORGE CAFFENTZIS is associate professor in the Department of Philosophy, University of Southern Maine, Portland, Maine (USA). A student of capitalist development, in recent years he has paid special attention to its impact on living conditions in Africa. His work includes *Abused Words, Clipped Coins and Civil Government. John Locke's Philosophy of Money* (New York, Autonomedia/Semiotext, 1989) and *Midnight Oil. Work, Energy, War, 1973–1992* (New York, Autonomedia, 1992), the result of joint work by the Midnight Notes Collective.

SILVIA FEDERICI, associate professor in International Studies and Political Philosophy at New College, Hofstra University, Hempstead, New York (USA), has made major contributions to the analysis of the female condition and social reproduction. More recently, she has been studying these issues in the African context. Her work includes *Il Grande Calibano. Storia del corpo sociale ribelle nella prima fase del capitale* (Milan, FrancoAngeli, 1984), co-authored with L. Fortunati.

ANDRÉE MICHEL, honorary director at the CNRS in France, is a scholar internationally known for her research on women and the family, especially in the developing countries. In recent years, she has linked these studies with research on the consequences of war and society's militarization on the condition of women. Her work includes: 'Multinationales et inégalités de classe et de sexe', in *Current Sociology*, 31, 1 (1983); 'La Militarisation et les violences à l'égard des femmes', in *Nouvelles Questions Féministes*, 11–12 (Winter, 1985) (editor); *Femmes et multinationales* (Paris, Karthala, 1981), co-authored with Agnès Fatoumata-Diarra and Hélène Agbessi-Dos Santos; *Le Féminisme* (Paris, Presses Universitaires de France, 1979) (third edition 1986, various translations); *Les Femmes dans la société marchande* (Paris, Presses

Universitaires de France, 1978)(collective work, also translated into Spanish).

ALDA BRITTO DA MOTTA is associate professor in the Department of Sociology and Centre for Interdisciplinary Studies on Women (Núcleo de Estudos Interdisciplinares sobre a Mulher, Mestrado em Ciências Sociais, NEIM), Federal University of Bahia, Salvador, Bahia (Brazil). Her focus is labour problems and the woman's condition, with special attention to female participation in politics. Her most important recent publications are *Espaço e Tempo de Mulher* (ed.) (Bahia, NEIM, 1987), Caderno do NEIM, No. 4; and *Familiarizando (-se com) o Publico e Politizando o Privado*, in Tereza Ximenes, (ed.), *Novos Paradigma e Realidade Brasileira* (Universidade Federal de Parà, 1993).

INAIA MARIA MOREIRA DE CARVALHO, associate professor in the Department of Sociology and the Human Resources Centre, Federal University of Bahia, Salvador, Bahia (Brazil), is a student of labour problems, pauperization, and urban social movements, with a special focus on women's political initiatives. Her most important recent publications are *O Nordeste e o Regime Autoritario* (São Paolo, Hucitec-Sudene Ed., 1987) and, with Ruthy Nadia Laniado, *A Sociedade dos Fatos Consumados,* Caderno CRH, No.17 (June–December 1992).

GIOVANNA FRANCA DALLA COSTA is professor in Industrial Sociology at the Faculty of Psychology, Department of General Psychology, University of Padua (Italy). Her field is the working conditions of women in relation to development issues. Her best-known works are: *Un lavoro d'amore. La violenza fisica componente essenziale del 'trattamento' maschile nei confronti delle donne* (Rome, Edizioni delle Donne, 1978), translated into Japanese as *Ai no Roudou* ('A Labour of Love') (Tokyo, Impact Shuppankai, 1991); *La Riproduzione nel sottosviluppo. Lavoro delle donne, famiglia e Stato nel Venezuela degli anni '70* (Milan, FrancoAngeli, 1989) (also Padua, Cleup, 1980).

MARIAROSA DALLA COSTA is associate professor in Political Sociology and professor of Comparative Politics at the Faculty of Political Sciences, University of Padua (Italy) and, at the same university, professor in the History of the Promotion of Woman's Condition at the Specialization School in Institutions and Techniques for Human Rights Safeguards. She has devoted her studies to woman's condition in capitalist development, social policies, and emigration/ immigration. Her best-known works include *The Power of Women and the Subversion of the Community* (Falling Wall Press, 1972) (also Padua, ed. Marsilio, 1972). This book, written with Selma James, was republished several times and translated into five languages. It opened the debate on housework in the early 1970s. Her more recent work includes *Famiglia, Welfare e Stato tra Progressismo e New Deal* (Milan, FrancoAngeli, 1983, 1992). A collection of her writings is available in Japanese: *Kajirodo ni Chingin-o Feminizumu no Aratana Tenbo* ('Wages for Housework, New Perspective for Feminism') (Tokyo, Impact Shuppankai, 1986 and second edition 1990).

TRANSLATIONS

The chapters by C. George Caffentzis and Silvia Federici were written in English. The chapter by Alda Britto da Motta and Inaiá Maria Moreira de Carvalho was translated from the Portuguese typescript by Cecilia Sardenberg and Sarah Hautzinger. The Introduction by Maria-rosa Dalla Costa and the chapters by Andrée Michel and Giovanna F. Dalla Costa were translated by Julian Bees from the Italian edition.

ABBREVIATIONS

ACP	African, Caribbean and Pacific (countries)
ADPs	Agricultural Development Projects
B	Bolivares
CEPAL	Economic Commission for Latin America and the Caribbean
CIA	Central Intelligence Agency
CLO	Civil Liberty Organization (Nigeria)
ECA	Economic Commission for Africa
EC	European Community
EP	European Parliament
GDP	Gross Domestic Product
GNP	Gross National Product
IDA	International Development Agency
ILO	International Labour Organization
IMF	International Monetary Fund
IPP	International Planned Parenthood
LDC	Least Developed Countries
NPP	National Population Policy (Nigeria)
NGOs	Non-governmental organizations
NEIM	Núcleo de Estudos Interdisciplinares sobre a Mulher, Mestrado em Ciências Sociais (Brazil)
OAU	Organization of African Unity
OECD	Organization for Economic Cooperation and Development
OPEC	Organization of Petroleum Exporting Countries
PNAD	National Domestic Unit Survey (Brazil)
SAP	Structural Adjustment Programme
TPP	Tribunale Permanente dei Popoli (Permanent People's Tribunal)
WIDE	Women in Development/Europe
UNFPA	United Nations Fund for Population Activities
UNICEF	United Nations Children's Fund
USAID	United States Agency for International Development
WAI	War Against Indiscipline (Nigeria)
WB	World Bank
WHO	World Health Organization
WIN	Women in Nigeria

1

INTRODUCTION

Mariarosa Dalla Costa

The essays published as chapters here are a partial reworking of reports submitted to a session on Women and the Economy that I chaired at the Twelfth World Congress of Sociology at Madrid, 9–12 July 1990. The first two chapters, by C. George Caffentzis and S. Federici, are the result of the authors' on-the-spot experience in Africa, where they worked for some years as lecturers respectively at Port Harcourt and Calabar universities.[1] When I visited Nigeria, and later, their work proved a precious guide.

Although there are some differences in approach, the book's common thread is the relationship between social reproduction and international debt policies in the socio-political reality of some African and Latin American developing countries. They all deal with the problem of pinning down more clearly the significance of the economic adjustment policies imposed by the International Monetary Fund (IMF) and the World Bank in the debt crisis.

Analysing the events of the last decade and the start of the present one, the authors, some more explicitly than others, argue that the purpose of these policies is not improvement, but rather a deterioration in the conditions of reproduction, with the result that increasingly large parts of the population face worsening impoverishment, in some cases even extinction.

Some contributors identify the new impetus given to these much wider social macro-operations as something very similar in form and intention to capital's first phase of 'primitive accumulation', the aim being to create a new foundation and stratification on a world-wide scale for a class condition characterized increasingly by few jobs, high unemployment, extensive precarious employment, and widespread denial of the conditions for survival.

Others may focus on the further deepening of the gap between North and South, with a yet heavier burden of even wider poverty among women and children. Social reproduction is seen, then, as a primary and

1

therefore fundamental terrain for the restructuring needed in a new phase of accumulation. For that reason in itself, social reproduction is the *object* and the *objective* of debt policies, yet at the same time the *subject* that renders more problematic the realization of these same policies. A subject that resists and continually restructures its relations – not in view of a 'promise of development', with a harvest of death and misery already amply revealed, but to realize a 'different kind of development' hailed by determined voices increasingly impossible to ignore in the most distant parts of the globe.

In social reproduction, the woman is the subject par excellence. Her condition is the index of the population's conditions of reproduction precisely because of her labour's critical position in maintaining family and community. This is all the more true in the so-called developing countries, where survival in very extensive areas depends primarily on the women working on the land, in craftwork, or in small retail activities – in other words, on women's informal labour, which is often even more important in these countries than housework.

A crucial focus of attention here is women's condition, not only because of the heavy pressure exerted because of the policies of the 1980s and early 1990s, which were increasingly harsh, but also because of women's own capacity for resistance, starting with the difference of their reproductive powers and their options on this terrain. Here state policies claim an increasingly 'official' right to interfere, imposing recipes that take no account of the population's interests *vis-à-vis* the real structures and forms on which social reproduction rests. The heart of the macro-processes characterizing Europe's primitive accumulation from the sixteenth to the eighteenth centuries was the policy of denying women, not only land and other subsistence resources, but also the power of control over their procreative capabilities (as well as their sexuality) in favour of male professionals and, in the last analysis, the state's power. In the same way, state control over fertility and birth rates continues to lie at the heart of the various structural adjustment programmes by which present-day policies seek to relaunch primitive accumulation at the world level today.

Since 1982, when the Mexican government declared a moratorium on debt payments and began what came to be known as the debt crisis, research from various disciplines has investigated the existence and significance of a relationship between debt and social reproduction policies – or more specifically, for our interests, between these policies and women's labour and struggles in Africa and Latin America. Three basic approaches have emerged.

The first, typical of the early 1980s, argues that the relationship is not systematically negative. The various adjustment policies are said to be the necessary consequence of governmental incompetence in managing resources; any adverse influences on social reproduction are an unintended side-effect. Moreover, if social reproduction is incidentally prejudiced, it will show progress later when, thanks to economic growth, the debt can be paid. This position is well illustrated in J. D. Sachs (1989), while the views of the International Monetary Fund (IMF), the World Bank and the international banks are summarized adequately in E. R. Freid and Ph. H. Trezise, eds (1989). The same position is also supported by A. MacEwan (1990), even if from a left-wing viewpoint critical of the IMF and the World Bank.

The second position rejects the suggestion that debt policies can be considered independently of their negative effects on social reproduction. It was particularly well documented and debated in the mid-1980s, when the effects of the first structural adjustment programmes in Africa and Latin America began to make their first, and dramatic appearance, with a deterioration in the indices for health, primary education, child and maternal mortality, and other significant measures of living conditions. Altogether, these effects were labelled as the 'social cost of adjustment'. Yet, while the existence of this factor was recognized, together with its effects on women's labour and the conditions of social reproduction, it was viewed as a necessary evil, and one that was not produced intentionally. An extensive literature arose on how to reduce the negative effects through forms of protection for the poor (Cornia, Jolly and Stewart, eds, 1989). The position also won support from IMF and World Bank officials, who proposed new loans in order to patch things up in health and education. This position, which we can dub the 'social cost' approach, finds expression in the works of S. George (1988), P. Korner *et al.*, eds (1986), P. R. Lawrence, ed. (1986), and K. J. Havnevik, ed. (1987). An important paper tracing the history of the IMF and the World Bank in order to explain the reasons underlying the 'social cost' approach is the one by W. L. Canak and D. Levi in J. F. Weecks, ed. (1989). The approach is also increasingly common in IMF and World Bank publications. The most exhaustive application of the 'social cost' approach to the African case is in the two volumes edited by B. Onimode (1989). Obviously, however, these few bibliographical references are purely indicative since the literature is very extensive.

The third position, rather than denying a systematic and negative relationship between debt policies and social reproduction, or assuming that the relationship is one of a necessary but transitional 'social cost', argues that the policies are expressly designed to transform social reproduction: the family's configuration, birth rates, educational indices, the sexual division of labour, land ownership and management, health, and so on. In fact, as the adjustment policies initially proposed as transitory or emergency measures became more and more clearly the definitive and ruling economic policy for Africa and Latin America, even the World Bank's theorists began presenting structural adjustment programmes as a 'chance' offered to the governments for a more 'efficient' reshaping of their social reproduction policies.

On this terrain, however, increasingly forceful grassroots movements have grown up and emerged. Unlike the anti-colonial and anti-imperialist movements of the past, they have formed around issues arising from living conditions and, as we have stressed above, are often led by women. In this sense, the increasingly explicit objectives that debt policies are designed to achieve have assumed a new role as *subjects* in the conflict that characterizes this era. By taking a redefinition of social reproduction as the specific aim of debt policies, the overall approach that emerges in this book provides a perspective that enables us to grasp who the main actors are – above all, women as the emerging protagonists in a struggle against those policies and the theory of development underpinning them.

For one thing, the theory offers a development imposed by the wealthy countries on the poor ones within the framework of a form of international cooperation that only benefits the former. For another, it not only imposes economic and cultural deprivation on the countries it afflicts, but is also a sinister source of war-mongering, generating the obligation of military rather than social expenditure as a function of further expansion of the debt. In short, it is a type of development in which the obligation is to strengthen and use a military apparatus as a contribution to the primitive accumulation that continually defines and separates out those in the world who have the right to live, those who can do nothing more than survive, and those who must die.

In the recent past, the political scenario has been changing with unusual speed, scope and frequency. Further changes relevant to the realities discussed here were registered as the book was in the translation and editing stage. In late 1992, Brazilian President Collor de Mello resigned shortly before the Senate began a debate to impeach him for corruption. In 1992, too, Venezuela saw repeated coup attempts by parts of the armed forces with support from sectors of the population against President Perez's economic policies. In Nigeria, the pro-democracy movement which is also battling the social expenditure cuts urged by the World Bank grew further: the protagonists organizing the various forms of resistance have been women, students, school and university teachers, and human rights activists. In education, in fact, the social expenditure cuts and the deterioration in educational structures resulting from the cultural policies demanded by the major financial agencies here as in Africa as a whole have left many students no other prospect than to give up their studies – and many teachers, their teaching. Against the struggles, initiatives and demands advanced by these parts of the population, the military regime has unleashed the heaviest of repressions.

These cases exemplify the rebellion of significant sectors of society against a model of development serving solely to extend the gap between the fewer countries that are getting richer and the increasing number getting poorer – in a daily battle with poverty, hunger, cultural deprivation and death to create a kind of growth whose corollary is corrupt and acquisitive bourgeoisies and bureaucracies, and an authoritarian repressive apparatus, military or otherwise.

In their study of the way in which this trend is continually redrawn and redirected by the major debt agencies, C. George Caffentzis and S. Federici work explicitly within the Marxian category of primitive accumulation. Normally, this describes the first phase of capitalist development when it served to deprive whole populations of their means of production and subsistence so that they could be turned into simple bearers of labour power alone, which they were therefore forced to sell in order to survive. But, as Caffentzis stresses at the start of his paper, this was not a one-off process; it returns whenever profits start falling and class power rises. In developing his analysis, Caffentzis sees the African population's resistance to capitalist discipline, which is also the root of the flight of capital from Africa, as a moment of strength for proletarians throughout the world – those who have had to abandon Africa in search of survival on the streets of the West, but just as much those from the West who are increasingly threatened by job- and social expenditure-threatening policies very similar to the ones being applied in the developing countries.

Within the framework of this argument, Federici explains how denial of the means of subsistence entails, primarily, dismantling the forms of community that ensure social reproduction in Africa through specific types of land management and control and child raising. The corollary of expropriation/privatization of the land is the creation of a Western-style 'one man, one wife; one couple, one child' nuclear family. This, according to government and World Bank officials, is a demographic transition that should in its own right open the gates to economic and social well-being. The author demystifies this assumption and analyses the complexity of the problems an African woman meets in her relations with these policies, her community, and the men belonging to it.

Arguing on a very similar wavelength, A. Michel looks at a development model imposed on Africa by the advanced countries in the light of the crucial role played by women's labour in sustaining the community. But it is precisely women and children who are hit first by so-called 'adjustment' policies. In a way very similar to what happened during the phase of primitive accumulation in Europe, they are, on one hand, increasingly excluded from previously available subsistence resources, especially land, and, on the other, denied access far more than men are to new resources, i.e. jobs. The worsening condition of women and children for the two periods considered, before and after the second Lomé Convention in 1979, is seen in economic, social and cultural terms. Nutritional, housing, environmental, health, and above all educational resources are reduced increasingly. According to the author, no radical change in these policies can be expected unless there is a substantial women's presence where political decisions are taken. But since the author is only too aware of the extent to which women's representatives in the upper institutional echelons can be conditioned by the political leadership they depend on, she urges a growth in women's and feminist grassroots movements and non-governmental women's associations – with all the limits these associations may show – in order to overturn the logic of the choices made so far.

In their analysis of the Brazilian case from the viewpoint of the problems typical of a type of growth productive of poverty rather than welfare, A. Britto da Motta and I. M. M. de Carvalho register a notable growth in collective movements for an improvement in neighbourhood conditions. In them, they find women as the emerging actors, by contrast with the traditionally limited participation of women in trade unions and parties. Initially, the authors claim, the position of women in the sexual division of labour, and therefore their sense of responsibility towards reproductive labour as wives and mothers, makes them take a role in initiatives to improve the local conditions of life. Subsequently, though, they extend their political participation and diversify into different spheres with the idea of contributing to a radical change in the proposed type of growth.

G. F. Dalla Costa's paper on Venezuela closes the volume. Outlining the attempted industrial take-off in the 1970s and giving a cross-section of this Latin American country in the crisis of the 1980s, her study finds some points of correspondence between what is happening there and what was observed in Nigeria. The correspondences are particularly significant for the emerging role being assigned to these countries within their respective continents. By the 1970s, Venezuela was supposed to become the leader of Latin American development, just as Nigeria was supposed to show the way in Africa. Instead, the 1980s was the decade of the *salto atras* (backward leap) from the hopes and partial achievements of the previous decades. Here too, with the dream of industrial take-off gone, the productive choices and social policies imposed by the IMF and the World Bank created a dramatic impoverishment of the population, increasing the percentage living below the absolute and relative poverty lines. A point made emphatically is that various international forums have now begun to make a more detailed analysis of, and to pay more careful attention to, the role that housework can play in the crisis. Patently clear in the directives emerging from these forums is an invitation to government policy makers to encourage the developing countries to redefine and reshape this type of labour in terms more appropriate to development and the surrogate role housework may play in the provision of social expenditure and services.

The author also stresses how these same forums are now pointing to the importance of, and need for, a requalification of the jobs women do outside the home for additional income. But, in the given state of impoverishment, requalification in fact corresponds to an intensification of labour, which women are less and less willing to accept. Moreover, policies encouraging a higher qualification of labour form a corollary to policies requiring the greater qualification/discipline of women overall, above all their greater civil and political participation. To succeed in preventing and controlling the population's growing rebellion against an austerity that is plunging it ever deeper into hunger – the Caracas and Merida bread price struggles in 1989 are significant examples – is the Venezuelan government's most immediate problem, as it is for governments in the developing countries in general. Here too, the emergence of a strong women's presence in the grassroots movements represents an increasingly problematic challenge for government attempts to apply the policies planned by the major financial agencies.

But, if more extensive and detailed attention is being given to housework in numerous international forums, and especially those most concerned with applying the debt policies imposed by the IMF and the World Bank, the slant of that attention is certainly incompatible with lightening the workload or enlarging life possibilities as the women's movement has been urging internationally. A good example of the views expressed in these forums is the recent report put out by the Group of Commonwealth Experts on 'women and structural adjustment'. The report asserts that effective adjustment requires the full participation of women. As producers, women's labour is critical to the output of food and labour-intensive manufactures, both of which are vital to the adjustment efforts, while their earnings are essential to contain the cuts in family income. Moreover, these income cuts, which currently form such a big part of adjustment, would have far worse effects on health and nutrition without women's domestic management and adjustment. The economic success of adjustment efforts and the minimization of social costs are critically dependent on the creative response of women. (*Engendering Adjustment for the 1990s* 1989: 18).

The authors of the document clearly do not consider a heavier burden of labour as a cost; for them, if anything, it is an expression of 'creativity'.

A radically different perspective has characterized the way in which women view their relationship with work since the development in the early 1970s of a movement in various advanced European and North American capitalist countries, contesting the idea that work related to reproduction should be unpaid and attributed solely to the female sex. This movement, and the debate it brought with it, soon spread beyond the areas where it originated. Unpaid labour as a typical burden of the woman's condition and a primary cause of her poverty has become an increasingly important issue in the political debate, especially among women. In addition, it now forms part of the analysis in various scientific disciplines. Needless to say, unpaid labour has also contributed a central moment of resistance and struggle in various parts of the world.

Perhaps one of the more important manifestations of this debate at the international institutional level occurred at the World Conference on Equality, Development and Peace held in Nairobi in 1985 to review and appraise the UN's Decade for Women. The conference agreed to modify Paragraph 120 of the document, *Forward-looking Strategies for the Advancement of Women*, so as to give adequate stress to unpaid labour. The final version of the paragraph thus reads:

> Recognition must be given to the remunerated and unremunerated contribution that women make to all aspects of development, and every effort needs to be made to identify, quantify and integrate this contribution in the government accounts, in economic statistics, and in the gross national product. Concrete steps must be taken to quantify the unremunerated contribution of women to agriculture, food production, reproduction and domestic activities (United Nations 1985).

Nevertheless, no mention is made of the recognition and quantification this contribution should receive as women's share of the national wealth they have contributed to producing.

In those years, the disasters into which the IMF's and the World

Bank's debt policies led a large part of the planet were so evident that they provoked the development of new analyses and forms of denunciation. Certainly worth mentioning is the session of the Permanent People's Tribunal held in Berlin in 1988, a session flanked and supported by vigorous street demonstrations against the two international agencies. The tribunal's ruling confirms: 'The global economy is dominated by the US, Japan, West Germany and the other members of the Group of Seven, their power pervades it. The Third World depression of the 1980s was largely caused by their policies' (TPP 1988: 22).

Eduardo Galeano's introduction to the ruling observes:

> Historically, the underdeveloped countries have been overwhelmed by the development of the developed countries; it is they who have been condemned to slavery by debt. The international financial police keeps watch on them and tells them what to do; habitually, it fixes the level of wages and public expenditure, investments and disinvestments, interest and customs tariffs, domestic taxes and all the rest, except the hour of sunrise and how often the rain falls.

One of the most striking statements quoted by Galeano is an observation from David Abdulah, a trade unionist from Trinidad and Tobago:

> They teach us that we cannot be masters of our destiny. Thus, the rich have no problem in exporting their crisis and can finance their modernization. The foreign debt is financing the West's second industrial revolution.

And Togba Nah Tipoteh, formerly a minister in Liberia and chairman of the African group of IMF and World Bank governors: 'It's the new colonialism. What does their policy in my country consist of? In reducing the production costs of the multinationals and increasing their rate of profit.' In the same vein, Tanzania's former Minister for Planning, Abdulrahman Babu: 'This policy implies worse crimes than those of colonialism.' And, in his analysis, Javier Mujica, an adviser to the Peruvian trade unions, argues that 'the international financial bodies should apply the international juridical norm defining and condemning genocide' (TPP 1988: 8–9).

Equally, the Tribunal has denounced the link between repression in the indebted countries and debt policy.

> And, even though it is true that there is no mention of the *desaparecidos* and the torture victims in the economic recovery plans, it is also true that they are their natural consequence. Those who plan the sacrifice of wages are not innocent of the consequent repression against the working-class movement (TPP 1988: 12).

Also, 'It is the people who finance the repression that strikes them and the waste that betrays them' (TPP 1988: 9). Again, the link between indebtedness and the militarization of development is denounced, as well as the functionality of militarization to the expansion of the debt. The document's appeal for disarmament is one of its most important points, and the ruling, which also mentions the numerous violations perpetrated by these policies against the fundamental rights of peoples and individuals as recognized in various international charters, concludes by calling for renunciation of the debt (TPP 1988: 24–6).

As regards women in particular, as we have seen, it is significant that, while various international bodies voice the hope that they will cooperate in managing these policies, the women who spoke out on this occasion in fact did so to denounce them as agents of genocide as well as of the destruction of the environment and its life forms. For India, Vandana Shiva argued: 'In the name of development, the IMF and the World Bank ... have violated natural cycles and laws, have destroyed woods and created deserts, have poisoned my soil, my water, my air. The Bretton Woods medicine is killing India.' Similar testimony comes from Ana Maria Fernandez of Paraguay: 'the World Bank is financing development projects that imply ethnocide against the indigenous community' (TPP 1988: 10–11).

The charges levelled against this type of development as a lethal nexus for creating poverty and destroying people and the environment were also the implicit theme of the Tribunal's session in Padua, 5–8 October, on 'The Conquest of America and International Law'. Again, Galeano writes in his *Five Hundred Years of Solitude*, one of the documents included in the session's acts:

> 12 October 1492 saw the birth of the reality that we are now living on a universal scale, a *natural order* which is the enemy of Nature, and a *human society* that describes only 20 per cent of humankind as 'humanity'.... The end of the century, the end of the millennium, a time for contempt. Few owners, many owned; few judges, many judged; few consumers, many that are consumed; few developed, many those that have been overwhelmed. And the few always fewer, the many always more, in every country and in the world.... This system which has turned unequal exchange into a world phenomenon was born five centuries ago, and has put a price on the planet and the human race. Since then, it has turned everything it touches into hunger and money. To live and survive, it needs a world that is organized unequally.... International law was engendered by the law of conquest (TPP 1992: 3–4).

The Tribunal's proposals once again included disarmament and, by way of a symbolic indemnity for the colonialist expropriation of the countries of the New World, the cancellation of the Third World countries' entire public debt, starting with those in Latin America and Africa.

But debt and what type of development have also become increasingly central themes in the debates of the various networks of women scholars who are active in studying the many aspects of human suffering, and militant in combating them. On one hand, there has been a growing world-wide awareness of how decisive these two factors are in determining the condition of women and their labour – and hence for social reproduction as a whole. On other hand, in their historical role of responsibility for reproduction, in many situations, women now represent the new outposts for interpretative insight, denunciation and initiative, in a reversal of priority from production to reproduction. This was one of the results achieved in the early days of the feminist movement of the 1970s, whence it has come to represent the starting point for other, above all ecological and pacifist movements in the 1980s and early 1990s. In these movements, the women usually represent the driving force.

One example of how women have started promoting a wide range of issues – converging around the rejection of a development which rests on war-mongering, sexism, racism, and the will to trample roughshod over Nature – is the debate at the World Women's Congress for a Healthy Planet at Miami in Florida on 8–12 November 1991. On that occasion, 1,500 women from 83 different countries tried to define an 'Ethical Code for a Woman-sized Earth'. This was summed up in an Action Plan for various areas. The plan's *Preamble: Toward a Healthy Planet* declared, in part:

> As caring women, we speak on behalf of those who could not be with us, the millions of women who experience daily the violence of environmental degradation, poverty, and exploitation of their work and bodies. As long as Nature and women are abused by a so-called 'free market' ideology and wrong concepts of 'economic growth', there can be no environmental security (United Nations 1991).

Apart from its condemnation of an international economic order that places capital before human and environmental welfare, the meeting took a stand on many areas of concern. They included the need to ensure protection for natural systems against exploitation in the name of the present model of development, to achieve a different orientation in science and technology, and to ensure that population-related policies are formulated in different terms. The various points give an important testimony of the extent to which these issues have been developed and the wide circulation they have received.

A number of them are worth highlighting as of more direct interest here. One is the condemnation of the expropriation of land for export crops as a primary cause of hunger among women and children, whence the demand for women's access to land possession and ownership rights as one of the basic human rights to be safeguarded. Then, there is the indignation expressed at the view that the female fertility rate, called euphemistically – as the conference noted – 'demographic pressure', is to be condemned. Describing the right to choice and education in procreation as a fundamental right for all individuals, the conference also warned that, according to World Fertility Survey estimates, there are as many as 500 million couples who want to plan their family, but have no access to the means, whence the request that resources for the healthy practice and legal regulation of fertility should be made available. All attempts to deprive women of their freedom of pro-creation or the knowledge needed to exercise that freedom are also condemned and, in another extremely important point, as part of the discourse on biotechnology and biodiversity, there is a recommendation against permission to patent life forms, so as to protect the South's genetic resources against commercial exploitation.

This last question brings us to a new process that the powers contrary to human happiness would like to set under way in the current phase of primitive accumulation. Not only is humankind expropriated of land and the other individual and collective rights that can guarantee survival in the developing and more industrial countries; not only are women (and men) expropriated of their ability to control their reproductive powers: the land itself is now expropriated of its reproductive powers so that they can be transformed into capital.

An increasingly monstrous domination faces us and is placing its stamp on our relationship with Nature – with all living beings, in inter-human relations, in relations between men and women. In the 1980s and early 1990s, the increasingly determined voices and actions of men and women have made themselves heard, geographically distant, perhaps, but close and convergent in their intent and practice around the real problem posed for all the movements: with the end of the present millennium, to write the word 'end' after the monstrous affair of conquest, not only of America, but of the Earth. Against the policies of suppression and silence, to grasp and spread the meaning of the experiences of such men and women as widely and extensively as possible is the task facing us in every forum where we can contribute to creating new paradigms and in every site of our activity.

Note

1. These chapters are also a product, as regards their analysis of the Nigerian case, of the research project 'Some aspects of social reproduction in the light of the crucial role of oil exports in Libya and Nigeria and oil imports in South Africa', directed by the present author and financed by a contribution from Cnr No. 87.01129.10.

Bibliography

Canack, W. L. and Levi, D. (1989). 'Social costs of adjustment in Latin America'. In Weeks, J. F. (ed.), *Debt Disaster? Banks, Governments and Multinationals Confront the Crisis*. New York: New York University Press.

Cornia, A. C., Jolly, R. and Stewart, F. (eds) (1989). *Per un aggiustamento dal volto umano*. Milan: Angeli.

Engendering Adjustment for the 1990s (1989). Report of a Commonwealth Expert Group on Women and Structural Adjustment. London: Commonwealth Secretariat.

Freid, E. R. and Trezise, Ph. H. (eds) (1989). *Third World Debt: The Next Phase*. Washington, DC: The Brookings Institution.

George, S. (1988). *A Fate Worse Than Debt*. New York: Grove Press.

Havnevik, K. J. (ed.) (1987). *The IMF and the World Bank in Africa*. Uppsala: Scandinavian Institute of African Studies.

Korner, P. *et al.* (eds) (1986). *The IMF and the Debt Crisis: a Guide to the World's Dilemma*. London: Zed Books.

Lawrence, P. R. (ed.) (1989). *World Recession and the Food Crisis in Africa*. London: James Currey.

MacEwan, A. (1990). *Debt and Disorder: International Economic Instability and US Imperial Decline*. New York: Monthly Review Press.

Onimode, B. (ed.) (1989). *The IMF, the World Bank and the African Debt*. London: Zed Books.

Sachs, J. D. (1989). *Developing Country Debt and Economic Performance*. Chicago: University of Chicago Press.

TPP (Tribunale Permanente dei Popoli) (1988). Ruling of the Session on 'Le politiche del Fondo monetario internazionale e della Banca mondiale'. Berlino ovest, 26–29 September 1988. Rome: Edizioni Associate.

TPP (1992). Ruling of the Special Session on 'La Conquista dell'America e il Diritto Internazionale'. Padova, 5–8 October 1992. Mimeographed document distributed by the Scuola di Specializzazione in Istituzioni e Tecniche di Tutela dei Diritti Umani of the Faculty of Political Sciences of the University of Padua.

United Nations (1985). 'Nairobi: forward-looking strategies for the advancement of women'. In *Report of the World Conference to Review and Appraise the Achievements of the United Nations Decade for Women: Equality Development and Peace*. Nairobi,

15–26 July 1985. United Nations publication (sales number E.85.IV.10).

United Nations (1991). *Women's Action Agenda 21, 1991.* In *World Women's Congress for a Healthy Planet, 8–12 November 1991, Miami, Florida, USA, Official Report.* New York: United Nations.

Weeks, J. F (ed.) (1989). *Debt Disaster? Banks, Governments and Multinationals Confront the Crisis.* New York: New York University Press.

2

THE FUNDAMENTAL IMPLICATIONS OF THE DEBT CRISIS FOR SOCIAL REPRODUCTION IN AFRICA

C. George Caffentzis

If we want to turn Africa into a new Europe ... then let us leave the destiny of our countries to Europeans. They will know how to do it better than the most gifted among us. But if we want humanity to advance a step further, if we want to bring it up to a different level than that which Europe has shown it, then we must invent and we must make discoveries.

Frantz Fanon (1963)

... any regime that can for one moment conceive of the intensification of colonialism as the way to save a Third World people from hunger has passed a verdict of damnation on itself. *Eskor Toyo (1986)*

A Common Assumption

The debt crisis generated an enormous amount of literature in the 1980s, and it would seem that little more can be added on a theoretical level to what has been written on this topic. I would argue, however, that much of this literature suffered from a major flaw, in so far as the analysts of both the Right and the Left viewed the debt crisis as an impediment to development and operated within a perspective for which capitalist development, either as a fact or as an ideal, is an un-questioned premise.[1] Certainly, there were differences concerning the specific threats which the debt crisis poses. The Right warned that a massive default on loan payments might jeopardize the very existence of the international banking system. The Left, instead, focused its atten-tion on the mismanagement of international credit by the commercial banks in the years of the 'petrodollar surplus', and stressed its contri-bution to the perpetuation of underdevelopment. Leftist economists also decried the ravages and suffering caused by the austerity measures which the IMF has imposed on debtor nations in order to force them to pay. However, with rare exceptions – H. Cleaver (1990), Sachs (1992) and Cheru (1989) for example – for both sides of the debate, the need for 'development' and 'economic growth' remains unquestioned.

This consensus is not surprising. Both in Europe and in North America the debate on the debt crisis has been carried on within a limited institutional setting, rarely moving beyond the confines of the commercial banks, the government circles, the international finance or aid agencies (IMF, World Bank, UN) and think tanks. Thus, except for the demonstration organized by an activists' coalition against the IMF summit in Berlin in September 1988 (*Commonsense* 1988), the debates rarely 'took to the streets' of Western Europe or the United States. And the voices of the people in the indebted countries, where anti-IMF demonstrations became a fact of political life, rarely made it directly into the official volumes; although the planetary *intifada* against the austerity regimes imposed under the cover of the debt crisis has been the dominant theme of insurrections, riots and demonstrations throughout Africa, the Caribbean and the Americas since the mid-1980s.[2]

This official literature had especially ignored the views of those who are most affected by the crisis (for example, women in the rural areas of indebted countries) and the resistance which the African proletariat has mounted against the expansion of capitalist relations in the region in particular. As I will argue, however, this official oblivion has precluded an understanding of the nature of the crisis and its implications for social reproduction in Africa.

What has remained unacknowledged is that the debt crisis and structural adjustment programmes (SAPs) imposed on heavily indebted governments by the IMF and the World Bank (WB) have been attempting to remould social reproduction in Africa. They are pivotal elements of a political and economic strategy which aims at radically restructuring class relations to make them more functional to the expansion of capitalism in Africa, irrespective of the cost to the African people. Privatization of state-supported companies, banking operations and services are only one aspect of this process. Equally important is the elimination of the last vestiges of communalism both in land property relations and in the organization of social reproduction, particularly in those spheres which most directly concern the production and repro-duction of labour power: the family, child-raising, male–female relations. For it is this communalism that has enabled Africans to resist the encroachment of capitalist relations to a degree unmatched in any other part of the world, which is the reason why developers and international finance agencies presently look at post-colonial Africa as a complete economic failure.

There is a tendency today to approach these communal 'remnants from the past' in a purely cultural or critical fashion, that is, either as anthropological curiosities or as signs of cultural backwardness. Africans seem to be fond of 'economies of affection', still to cherish 'peasant values', or to be cursed by 'perverse, backward-bending labour supply curves'.[3] For in so far as capitalist relations are assumed to be 'natural laws', any society whose organization contradicts (capitalist) rationality appears to be out of step with the times. Thus, political economists, even when they recognize that behind the decline in the profit rate in post-colonial Africa there is a history of social struggles, do not view these as anti-capitalist struggles, and search instead for novel sociological categories – such as the 'semi-proletarianized peasantry' (Arrighi and Saul 1973) or the 'uncaptured peasantry' (Hyden 1985) – to explain phenomena that are by no means anomalous, if we admit that just and reasonable alternatives can exist to capitalist conceptions of life. Indeed, it would be unreasonable for Africans not to resist having to pay rent on lands which they consider their own, or having to repay loans which they did not contract, or having to settle for wages not even sufficient for subsistence. We need not resort to anthropological stereotypes concerning a supposed 'African nature' to account for the difficulties which the expansion of capitalist relations encounters in Africa. Africa's 'failure to develop' in the post-colonial period should be seen as the expression of a desire on the part of a broad stratum of Africans for a different form of 'modernization' from the one offered by international bankers and development agencies in Washington, London or Paris.

Viewing the motives for debt crisis and the resistance to SAPs in this perspective enables one to explain a number of apparent anomalies, which the standard analyses of Right and Left fail to account for. For example:

- Why do the SAPs imposed on debtor African countries by the international banks and agencies continue to be pursued long after they have have proved unable to accomplish their supposed task: debt reduction?

- Why do international agencies continue to loan to debtor nations in Africa, although admittedly there is no likelihood that the borrowed money will be repaid in the foreseeable future?

Indeed, from a narrowly economic viewpoint the IMF/WB loan

policy itself appears irrational, for the decade-long regime of SAPs which was officially intended to reduce the debt has actually increased it.[4] But the policy *is* quite rational, *if* we see the loaning process as a mechanism used to intervene in crucial areas of social life, and we understand the debt crisis as a strategy by which international capital is again trying to 'modernize' Africa. That is, the IMF/WB strategy is a long-term effort to make Africa more profitable for capital investment, a process which involves both completing the privatization of African land and eliminating the last remnants of communal social relations. Put in Marxist terms, the debt crisis is a means by which a new phase of original or primitive accumulation is being activated in the African continent. In this perspective the success of the IMF/WB policies presently adopted is not to be measured in terms of their immediate monetary returns, but in terms of their ability to reshape social reproduction and to make the production and expenditure of labour power more functional to the needs of international investors and the international labour market.

Original Accumulation as an Analytic Category

Marx employs the notion of original or primitive accumulation to account for the historicity of capitalist relations, to argue, in other words, that they have an origin and an end. Capitalist class relations are not eternal; they have a genesis and need to be revitalized through the continual separation of masses of humans from the means of reproduction in order to be able to exploit and appropriate their surplus labour. Marx's reference model for this process was the English enclosures that expropriated the land with 'fire and blood' from the agricultural population between the sixteenth and eighteenth centuries.[5] But primitive accumulation is not a one-time, one-place affair. Whenever the profit rate tendentially falls and workers' power over the means of production and reproduction rises, the launching of a new phase of the primitive accumulation process is potentially at hand. Primitive accumulation was re-enacted in the British Isles after the defeat of the Scottish clans in 1745, with the clearances of the Highlands, as well as after the defeat of the 'native Irish' during the Cromwellian and Williamite War of the seventeenth century; it has proceeded in step with the 'transition to capitalism' in most of Western Europe; and before this it was launched on a much larger scale, with the expulsion of the indigenous people from their lands in the Americas. Both in Europe and in the Americas primitive accumulation has been a sort of 'eternal return'. Indeed the *lebensraum* ideology of the Third Reich can be in part seen as a 'rationale' for a new phase of primitive accumulation, this time subjecting Europeans to the same violent expropriation of land and 'social rights' that had been standard in the colonized world. Genocide, starvation, mass forced migrations, wars of extirpation and plagues are, of course, the violent symptoms of the most fundamental 'liberation' of labour power which is known as primitive accumulation.

In the case of Africa, we can note two phases in the primitive accumulation of African labour. The first coincided with the Atlantic slave trade (1650–1800), when Africans were brought as slaves to the Americas after their means of reproduction had been forcibly expropriated by kidnapping, legal punishments, and war.[6] The second coincided with colonialism proper (1880–1930), when the means that were employed to expropriate Africans were taxes, corvée and land seizures (Sender and Smith, 1986b). The fiscal recolonization of the African countries and the diaspora of African labour that have been activated by the debt crisis represent the third phase of primitive accumulation in Africa, once again introduced to separate Africans from their land and social relations.

However, the expropriation of the means of reproduction and subsistence does not involve only the expropriation of the land. At the core of social reproduction in a capitalist society is the reproduction of labour power; and historically, as Federici has shown (Federici and Fortunati 1984; Federici 1988b and 1992), this has implied the attempt by the state to control demographic rates and therefore women's procreative and sexual activity. In other words, primitive accumulation involves also the expropriation of the body, of sexual and reproductive powers, in so far as they are means for the accumulation of labour – an outstanding example of this process being the sixteenth- and seventeenth-century witch hunts which, through the institution of an unprecedented regime of terror, expropriated women of control over their reproductive activity, paving the way for state control of demographic rates and the accumulation of labour (Federici and Fortunati 1984; Federici 1988b; Mies 1986).

If we apply this multi-dimensional understanding of primitive accumulation to an examination of the consequences of the debt crisis for social reproduction in Africa, we see that we are witnessing a new capitalist accumulation of land and bodies as well as resistance to it.[7] This approach departs from that of 'dependency theory' or 'mode of production' theory, which focus respectively on the 'unequal exchange' between the metropolitan and peripheral areas of the world market and the consequences of the alleged absence of capitalist relations in the

'Third World', neither of which is capable of accounting for the dynamic character of the crisis. For the strategy here is to completely remould the 'dependent partner' or the 'pre-capitalist mode of production.'

The Wage–Profit Crisis in Post-colonial Africa

Sub-Saharan Africa glaringly shows the difficulty of understanding the debt crisis in the traditional terms of capitalist development and under-development. First, the impact of Africa's combined foreign debt is only a small fraction of the total $1.3 trillion debt of Third World countries. As of 1987, sub-Saharan African debt was $109 billion (IMF 1989). If sub-Saharan African governments repudiated their debt tomorrow, the effect of this default on the international banking system would be rather limited. The often cited $500 billion impact of the Savings and Loan crisis in the US (White 1991) dwarfs the total 1987 sub-Saharan African debt five times over. In the case of the African debt, moreover, the creditors are quite diverse and include not only the US but the Japanese government, the Western European governments and Russia.

Why, then, is there so much interest in Africa and its debt? Clearly there is an interest in the mineral wealth of Africa. The debt gives more leverage to the exploitation by creditor nations of these minerals as state mining companies are privatized and debt-for-equity swaps give international banks stock in these companies. But both the IMF and WB agree that at the root of the debt crisis in Africa is a wage–profit crisis that has structural roots stemming from the organization of Africa's social relations. As the WB claims:

> the low return on investment is the main reason for Africa's recent decline … wage costs are high relative to productivity (particularly in the CFA franc zone), even though real wages have fallen by about a quarter on average across Africa since 1980 (World Bank 1989a).

Absolutely, and in comparison to the South Asia area, the post-independence era has shown a dramatic decline in the rate of return on investment in Africa (table below).

Region	1961–73	1973–80	1980–7
Sub-Saharan Africa	83.8	23.5	6.2
South Asia	47.8	38.5	36.5

Source: World Bank 1989a: 26.

What lies behind this phenomenon? Why is investment in Africa 'uncompetitive' on the international capital market? The WB sums it up in two terms: 'poor public resource management' and 'bad policies'. We also hear of an 'unfavourable environment to investment'. But, since the root of profitability is to be found in the labour process, the key issue is identified in a collection of essays edited by Ron Lesthaeghe, where it is claimed that the peculiarity of the African relation to development stems from the survival in every aspect of reproduction of communal relations (Lesthaeghe 1989b: 1–59) and specifically:

- The relation many Africans still have to the means of subsistence. Even in the context of urbanization, access to land is still communally organized to an extent unknown in the rest of the planet. Although communalism is not necessarily synonymous with egalitarianism (women are in many cases excluded either in principle or *de facto* from land entitlements) access to land is often considered one's 'birthright', and remains a birthright even if one leaves the village and goes to an urban centre or emigrates to Europe or the US. This situation has made urban African workers more combative, and has posed a constant challenge for developers.

- The relation that Africans have to the family, marriage and child-raising. The African family is not based on the dyadic spousal relation and the Oedipal parent–child bond that characterize the nuclear family and are considered a standard of 'transition' demography (W. Goode 1963; Caldwell 1990). In Africa the extended family is still prevalent. Polygyny and even polygamy are practised to a degree that is anomalous even with respect to Islamic Asia. Although gender relations are patriarchal, the spousal relation is weak and plural, as women and men live in separate economic spheres, and child-raising is communally organized. One characteristic of the African family is the 'circulation' of children who, depending on the need, are distributed throughout the body of the extended family, in a way that precludes a vertical transmission of property and discipline. As Page points out (1989), the situation of Africa is paradoxical: despite the immense value that is attributed to children and the strong tie between parents and children, there is a great willingness to have them raised by other members of the family. The rights and responsibilities with respect to the children are not only 'shared', but they can be 'transferred'; they are not only delegated (to), but they are taken over by other family members. As the Mende of Sierra Leone say, 'a child is not for one person' (Lesthaeghe 1989c:

402). Children belong to all the members of the lineage. Thus, in the villages, it is at times difficult to understand who has the responsibility to feed them, since they wander from the pot of one relative to that of another; and few Africans feel less responsibility with respect to the schooling of their nephews than they feel towards the schooling of their own children (Caldwell and Caldwell 1990: 207). The possibility of 'distributing' children through the body of the extended family also implies a lesser preoccupation with extramarital births and sexual relations (Lesthaeghe 1989b: 24–6).

In sum, communalism, although eroded by the spreading of 'modernization', still shapes the reproduction process, with many consequences for the type of social discipline investors and developers consider necessary to the creation of a congenial and profitable business environment. For the continuation of the extended family and communal relations in land-holding and family life has meant that the typical African has in the past been able to rely upon access to some land and the support of a family network that allowed him or her to resist speed-ups, unemployment threats, and even military intimidation. Although these communalist relations are not antithetical to capitalism (many communal farmers produce for the market, even the international one) their responses to capitalist stimuli, both locally and internationally, are unpredictable.

This unpredictability penetrates into African capital itself. For, according to P. Kennedy, the prevalence of communal relations has even had an impact on business management (Kennedy 1990). Frequent complaints, for example, in catalogues of the reasons why Africa lacks a 'favourable business climate' are that:

- African managers are too subject to pressures from below – for instance, they feel obliged to hire people whom they know, above all relatives, independently of their capacities;

- They do not have sufficiently the sense of private enterprise and therefore rarely give the management of their business to non-members of the extended family;

- Social stratification is not yet sufficiently defined (Kennedy 1990: Chapter 7).

The Debt Crisis as a Productive Crisis

This 'primitive accumulation' conception of the debt crisis and SAPs in Africa puts into question much of the discourse concerning causes and consequences, especially the often used charge of 'failure'. For example, in the literature on the debt crisis it has often been claimed that the banks and international lending institutions have *failed* to monitor adequately the loan requests by Third World nations and to approve projects only after they were proved feasible, that is, capable of paying their way and providing a 'sensible' return (George 1988; Payer 1982). On the other hand, debtor governments and élites are charged with *failures* of administration: corruption, bad planning and poor management skills (Korner *et al.* 1986). In turn, the post-1982 attempts of the IMF and WB to counter the debt crisis with SAPs are dismissed as *failures* since they violate national sovereignty, put the burden of adjustment on the weaker social classes and promote political instability (Loxley 1987). Finally, African leaders and people are told that they have *failed* to 'face reality' and have been living beyond their means (*Africa Research Bulletin* 31 July 1989).

But in order to assess the 'failure' of a policy one must know its intent. Surely, in terms of debt reduction, the more than 30 SAPs that have been installed in sub-Saharan Africa since 1980 have been failures? Instead of debt reduction, there has been, in the most important cases, a debt increase. In the key country of Nigeria, for example, the foreign debt has increased from about $18 billion at the beginning of the debt crisis in 1982 to $32 billion in 1990. For sub-Saharan Africa as a whole, the annual increase of long-term debt has been on the average of 20 per cent a year in the period 1985–90, while the ratio of external debt to exports has increased nearly twofold, from 178.6 in 1981 to 338.2 in 1990 (IMF 1989). Even between 1990 and 1991 the African debt as a whole increased from $161 billion in 1990 to $176 billion in 1991 (World Bank 1991). Indeed, the only debt reductions throughout the continent have been accomplished by commercial banks 'writing off' some debts and governments cancelling others. One cannot claim, then, that monetarist policies sponsored by IMF/WB officials and driven by 'free market forces' have led to any economic turnaround in the indebted countries. Between 1980–85, when the bulk of the SAPs were put into place, and the present, there has been negative growth in the *per capita* gross national income for most of the region (*Africa Research Bulletin* 31 December 1989). This has been especially disconcerting since in the latter half of the 1980s the OECD countries

substantial GNP growth, potentially making their markets more recep-
tive to African exports. Thus it would appear that the IMF/WB
approach to the debt crisis has been a dismal failure. But an admission
of failure from these institutions can hardly be expected. In 1989
Charles Humphreys and William Jaeger of the WB were still defending
the SAP record in Africa, by distinguishing between countries with
'strong' and 'weak' reform programmes:

> Excluding countries recently affected by weather, terms of trade, and other
> exogenous shocks (both positive and negative), annual GDP growth rates
> in reforming countries accelerated on average from just over 1 percent
> during 1980–84 to almost 4 percent on average in 1986 and 1987. By
> contrast, the growth rates in countries with weak or no reform programs
> increased only a third as much in 1986 and 1987 (Humphreys and Jaeger
> 1989).

These claims were challenged, however, by the United Nations Economic Commission for Africa (ECA), a frequent antagonist of the
IMF/WB. The ECA disaggregated the World Bank figures and showed
that if one looked at those for a selected group of 'strong' and 'weak'
reform countries the results would negate those of Humphreys and
Jaeger (*Africa Research Bulletin* 31 October 1989).

But the most telling refutation of the Humphreys-Jaeger argument
came from the IMF and WB in their 1989 reports on debt and Africa.
Two IMF officials, Dooley and Watson, took a sceptical attitude towards
the 'strong' SAPs lauded by their WB colleagues. They argued that by
early 1989 the most deeply indebted countries were caught in a
pernicious cycle of rising debt and poorer prospects for growth:

> [for] many debtor countries judged the likelihood of working their way out
> of debt, even with reasonably good policies, to be diminishing. Commercial
> banks had already indicated, by building reserves against loan losses
> (provisioning), and by selling loans at deep discounts in the secondary
> market, that they also regarded the future economic performance of some
> debtor counties as highly uncertain. Each year that registered a further build
> up of debt, without any conviction that there had been a decisive improve-
> ment in the prospects for sustained growth, could reduce the likelihood of
> any return to normal access to credit markets for indebted countries
> (Dooley and Watson 1989).

Dooley and Watson argued that the debt strategy needed to be
'reinvigorated' by accommodating more debt reduction and curtailing
the rescheduling agreements. This new turn came in the wake of an
admission by the IMF staff that it had made a mistake. In 1985 the IMF
had projected a significant drop in the debt–export ratio in countries

with debt-servicing problems, from 256 per cent in 1984 to 185 per cent in 1988. But events proved it wrong; by 1988 the ratio was 278 per cent. Dooley and Watson had no doubts: '[T]he discrepancy reflects misjudgments about the evolution of the terms of trade, the rate at which real exports would expand, and exchange rate changes' (IMF 1989). This time the World Bank joined in the *mea culpa*, admitting that:

> Responsibility for Africa's economic crisis is shared. Donor agencies and foreign advisers have been heavily involved in past development efforts along with the African governments themselves. Governments and donors alike must be prepared to change their thinking fundamentally in order to revive Africa's fortunes (World Bank 1989a: 2).

Indeed, the 1989 World Bank Report on Africa, *From Crisis to Sustainable Growth,* raises questions which signalled a departure from the Berg report's earlier arrogant neo-liberal apriorism (World Bank 1981). The 1989 Report asked, for example, whether Africa faces special structural problems that have not been properly understood; whether the institutional dimension has been neglected; whether the recent reform programmes have been too narrowly conceived. Could the formulation and implementation of reforms be improved? The questioning deepened in 1992 when a WB researcher, Ibrahim A. Elbadawi, concluded that not only did SAPs in Africa not reduce the debt burden, but they actually inaugurated a decline in investment and economic growth (Elbadawi 1992). Yet, even their own expressions of failure did not deter the IMF and the WB from pursuing their SAP policies. Nor was the WB deterred by the criticism of the *Wall Street Journal,* which has persistently editorialized against the granting of any more loans or aid to sub-Saharan Africa, until the region's population 'can learn' that capitalist development is their only path of survival. On the contrary, one of the leading officials of the WB, Lawrence Summers (now in the Clinton administration), reaffirmed the commitment to SAPs in late 1992 even though he admitted that though 'adjustment lending has been effective in reducing macro imbalances and restoring some growth, the basic development problems have not been solved' (Summers and Pritchett 1993: 388). Obviously some objective was being achieved that did not appear in the monetary indexes, since the IMF and WB are capitalist institutions *par excellence* and not dispensers of grace. What can explain IMF and WB behaviour and their increasing neglect of the official reason for SAPs in the first place, debt reduction?

The debt crisis and subsequent SAPs have helped to lay the ground-work in Africa for a historic expropriation in the areas of land and reproduction. In the post-colonial period the African governments, under immense pressure from their populations, initiated a process of indigenization and redistribution of land, while promoting expansionary demographic policies through increasing investment in health and education (Okoth-Ogendo 1980; Binswanger and Deininger 1993). For with the departure of the colonial powers and armies, it was difficult for the African state to directly resist mass economic demands. To this day some read the prevailing presence of authoritarian rule as a sign of loss of control over production and reproduction (Jackson and Rosberg 1985).

Since the debt crisis and the imposition of the SAPs, there have been policy reversals throughout the region. Land policies are being rewritten, increasingly allowing for foreign ownership and privatization of tenure, while demographic policies are now restrictive, aiming at the elimination both of the older forms of diffused family responsibilities and of the newer demand by women for more control over their reproductive activity. These policy changes are intended to affect the micro-structure of African society, activating the primitive accumulation of the African proletariat both in Africa and, through a 'second diaspora', in Europe and North America.[8]

The debt crisis and the IMF/WB policies and programmes have put African land and sexuality increasingly in the hands of international capital. This transformation has not been accomplished without a major struggle which is by no means over. But the present IMF/WB offensive has used the debt crisis to put into crisis not only the financial structures of African governments, but, more crucially, the attempt of the anti-colonial movement to chart a new path for social and economic life in Africa. Certainly the prophetic words of Fanon are being realized, and the second post-colonial generation is reaping the storm of decisions made at the beginning of the revolution. Once more the African ruling classes and officialdom are 'leaving the destiny [of Africa] to Europeans' and it is only those at the bottom that are making the 'inventions' and 'discoveries'.

The New Enclosure Movement

The historic basis for proletarian resistance to capitalist exploitation has been the ability to control land use. This point is frequently forgotten when it is argued that perpetuating the existence of the village is a means for capital to eschew the costs of workers' reproduction. This might be true in the 'labour reserve' economies of Southern Africa, but the existence of the village and the right of usufruct is also a source of power against exploitation, which can subvert the dream of developmental planners – W. A. Lewis's model of 'unlimited supplies of labour' (Lewis 1958). Thus the village and 'land tenure' relations are central to the wage–profit crisis in Africa, keeping in mind that land tenure rules and practices in sub-Saharan Africa are often a complex and contradictory mixture of customary land rules, Islamic maxims, colonial precedents and post-colonial decrees, all simultaneously operating (as in the case of Nigeria's middle belt). Thus it may not be appropriate to discuss land usage in many parts of Africa in terms of 'tenure', since in much of Africa there is still a tradition of *unsettlement*, to which every new attempt at 'modernization' only adds a further level of complexity. The historic 'settlement' of the land question has not happened in sub-Saharan Africa in the way it has in Europe (through the expropriation of the communal land), or in the Americas and Australia (through the genocidal expropriation of the indigenous peoples), or in Asia (where pre-capitalist state forms had set relatively stable land tenure rules). This is what distinguishes the operation of structural adjustment policies and the debt crisis in Africa, compared, for example, to South America.

Private property in land has yet to become an ontological given in much of Africa as it has in the rest of the planet. Karl Polanyi's 'great transformation' has not been completely accomplished, and in some areas has actually been reversed. This characteristic of African proletarian life can easily be romanticized, and indeed, when it comes to land tenure, experts rely on an anthropological terminology which hides the reality of a use-based system of tenure.[9] But there is no doubt that it is a source of preoccupation for those analysts who look at the world from a capitalist viewpoint. As the London *Economist* argued, in an investors' report on Nigeria of 1986, it is a generally held belief in investment circles that no capitalist development can occur in a country until the land question is settled and land property is privatized (London *Economist* 1986). Decolonization has further unhinged land tenure claims, by putting the former colonialists' lands in legal limbo (Pankhurst and Jacobs 1988; Davison 1988b).

Thus, one aim of the debt crisis is to put an end to this 'land scandal'. For as long as a communal, use-based relation to land exists, the process of urbanization and the current diaspora of African labour will not be subject to capitalist control and African labour will not be accumulated by either local or international capital. The debt crisis makes this attack on the 'land scandal' possible in two ways: by increasing land expropriation by international agencies, foreign interests and government officials; and by privatizing agriculture in the 'peasant' sector, and promoting the formation of a class of small landowners and capitalist 'farmers'. Almost all SAPs make provisions for increased foreign ownership of land, and the WB is often a part owner of expropriated land for agricultural projects (Whitaker 1988: 203). Indeed, the WB openly made its commitment to the commoditization of land in its 1989 *From Crisis to Sustainable Growth* where it clearly called for changes in the land laws of African governments:

> As population increases and land becomes scarce, long fallow periods can no longer be relied on to maintain fertility, and the transitory nature of land-use fails to provide incentives for individuals to improve their land ... [permanent titling will] help rural credit markets to develop, because land is good collateral (World Bank 1989a: 104).

The debt crisis did not initiate the effort to 'settle the land question', which had already begun prior to the 1980s; but it has accelerated its pace. In Sudan, for example, in the 1970s the WB encouraged the government to expropriate large amounts of land for the mechanization of cotton production. At the same time, Saudi and Arab capital took control of several millions of acres in the Blue Nile Province in order to expand rain-fed mechanized farming that was presumably to turn Sudan into the 'breadbasket' of the Arab world (Faaland 1987; Timberlake 1986). However, contrary to forecasts, this expropriation has led to famines and to a land war that has been falsely characterized in the international media as a religious struggle between the Islamic North and the 'animist' South (Korner *et al.* 1986; O'Brien 1986).

Similarly, huge tracts of land have been expropriated by state officials in projects sponsored by the WB and other international agencies in Zaïre. This type of 'development' has enriched the Zaïrean state bourgeoisie, which, upon realizing that the 'bush' could be turned into a source of wealth, was able with the help of the WB to use the state apparatus to expropriate land and then privately buy it, leading to an African gentrification. By 1975 a Zaïrean village elder, responding to a 'green revolution' maize programme in Shaba, expressed the widespread suspicion of these schemes: 'We have been developed and developed so many times that we don't believe any of the promises. We are tired of being developed' (Schoepf 1986).

By the mid-1980s, however, with the debt crisis giving the WB and IMF more leverage, this double land expropriation from both foreign and domestic holders of capital was leading not just to a weariness with 'development'. For the IMF and WB privatization plans have a hidden agenda, as an acute observer of the Zaïrean situation noted:

> Privatization draws legitimacy from the view that since capitalist and

peasant agriculture are discrete, unrelated 'sectors', policy measures favouring capitalist interests will not affect the peasants – or, alternatively, will provide employment for surplus rural labour. Seldom is it acknowledged that policies favouring large farm interests simultaneously tend to worsen the already miserable condition of the peasantry. When a major share of resources are allocated to capitalist development, peasants, as a class, are not just neglected. They are harnessed to provide the dominant class with capital, labour and land (Schoepf 1986).

The origin, therefore, of the Zaïrean debt crisis is not only the local 'cleptocracy' and the 'impotence' of the IMF to control the Mobutuist state, as Korner *et al.* claim (1986). On the contrary, corruption and lack of direction have been functional for the accumulation of class relations.

[R]esponding to IMF demands for budget cuts to reduce deficit spending the central government provides few resources to peripheral areas.... In the name of decentralization, local administrations have levied new taxes on peasants and traders, while decontrol of rural producer prices has benefited largely the traders. Devaluation has raised prices of tools and consumer goods (Schoepf and Schoepf 1988).

We are frequently told that Mobutu's private fortune, which is stored in foreign banks and investments, is greater than Zaïre's national debt; yet we can be sure that were Mobutu to pay the debt, his gesture would not be welcomed by international capital, since the existence of the debt is far more crucial to the future of capitalism in Africa than its payment.

A similar form of IMF/WB-sponsored land expropriation is taking place in the West African savanna region (including Mali, Senegal, Niger, Nigeria and Burkina Faso). S. P. Reyna (1987) has shown that international donors (from the EEC to the WB) have continually urged the Burkinabe post-independence governments to create state corporations that would expropriate the traditional land users and give a start to large-scale export-oriented agriculture. Reyna concludes:

the evidence suggests that the development investment policies of Western donor countries contributed to three Burkinabe land-concentration processes in the 1960s and 1970s. Further, each process either removed or gave control over land to individuals, facilitating different aspects of class formation. [This] expropriation removed land from many ordinary farmers and helped to create a semiproletariat. State corporation appropriation gave few officials control over considerable land, thus contributing to the emergence of class relations based on state coerced cash-cropping. Private appropriation gave certain élite persons, often officials, control over land, thereby facilitating the development of agrarian capitalist class relations (Reyna 1987: 532).

The debt crisis in the 1980s has given a further impetus to this process. Indeed, one sees in the insistence on the application of SAP-type policies in such a fragile 'low-income' country as Burkina Faso a totalitarian will for the triumph of capitalist relations everywhere, whatever the cost may be. And the 1987 assassination of Captain Thomas Sankara, the leader of the Burkinabe revolution, showed that no resistance to this process would be tolerated, even on an ideological level.

The primitive accumulation of an African proletariat can be seen best in Africa's most populous country, Nigeria. The huge international land grabs, as in Bakalori and in the WB agricultural development projects, have fuelled an extensive land war over an increasingly diminished arable area. The new development in the context of the SAP privatization policies in Nigeria and elsewhere is a shift from state corporations to the further stimulation of a bureaucratic gentry which has 'a keener appetite for land' with the increased prices for food crops (Toyo 1986). This is leading the rural population into the following situation: 'the overwhelming majority are semiproletariat on their own lands, others are tenants on state corporation lands, or labourers on bureaucratic or merchant farms' (Reyna 1987: 536).

Thus, although the IMF/WB claim that the new emphasis on 'higher food prices' and the privatization of agriculture shifts the balance from the urban to the rural population, its consequences work in the opposite direction. Such policies connect land claims more directly to the production of cash crops and make the holding of regularized land claims more profitable. Thus the main effect of the IMF/WB price revolution on African agriculture is not to increase the price of crops *per se*, but to put a price on African land. When this is achieved, the state bourgeoisie is then tempted to intervene and settle the land question by transforming itself to gentry. Indeed, gentrification is now in Africa, as it was in eighteenth-century England, the necessary complement of enclosure.[10]

Sexual-Social Reproduction:
Malthus, Debt, AIDS and Infibulation

The second success of the debt crisis is in the African body, a male/female body of mythic dimensions in the imagination of economic analysts. For the economic consequences activated by the debt crisis and SAPs have given legitimacy to their attempt to control African sexuality. While in the first post-colonial years European/American leaders would have refrained from making pronouncements concerning the sexual behaviour of Africans, especially when delivering them on the continent, by 1984 A. W. Clausen (then president of the WB) felt no qualms about informing the Kenyan Family Planning Programme that the Bank was taking initiatives to reduce the fertility of Africa's poor in the heart of Nairobi.

> During the next five years, the number of population and related health projects that we plan to finance in sub-Saharan Africa will rise to twenty-one from a total of three financed by the Bank in the five years to mid-1983. And the number of countries of the region which will be borrowing from us for that purpose will likely rise from three to seventeen (Clausen 1986).

This time the Bank's message was listened to without demur, not surprisingly, in a year when the debt–export ratio in sub-Saharan Africa was inching up more than 20 per cent due to drought and the fall of commodity prices. In the same year, the majority of representatives at the second African Population Conference, held in Arusha, came out in support of the WB's anti-natalist policies. At that time, in presenting the demographic transition view of 'fertility reduction', Clausen called for a 'social contract' between African governments and African parents, with the governments providing economic and social opportunities (secure future, access to education, health and family planning services) and the parents limiting their family size.[11] He did not explain, however, how African governments could propose such a 'social contract', when three years of their export earnings were tied up in external debt and the debt service–export ratios were reaching debt bondage levels. Instead, Clausen ended his speech on an anti-malthusian note, confidently stating that while the world population had grown to higher numbers than Malthus would ever have imagined, so had world production and incomes. If only governments could correct the present mismatch between population and income-producing ability – he added – the doomsday outcome that Malthus had seen as inevitable would be avoided (Clausen 1986).

But while the voiced message was one of hope and choice, in practice the WB and other financial agencies have managed the debt crisis in such a way as to create a strikingly malthusian situation, characterized by the presence of 'positive' and 'negative' checks: famines, war and disease, generated by falling incomes, reduced health services and changes in land tenure and cropping. Indeed, the African body, especially the female body, has been attacked by starvation, despair and plague rumours, in ways similar to those in which the European proletariat in the 'transition to capitalism' was terrorized by witch hunts, plagues of syphilis, the 'price revolution', famines and war. The outcome of this campaign cannot be presented in traditional economic indices: GNP, interest rates or foreign exchange values. At best we can look at demographic statistics and note that, starting in 1982, there has been a reversal in the post-colonial decline in African mortality. Since 1983, a number of sub-Saharan countries have seen an actual increase in crude death rates. Similarly infant mortality, after a general decline in the 1960–80 period, has begun to rise in the period between 1981 and 1989 in five out of 22 sub-Saharan countries, while remaining stagnant in another five. The increase in life expectancy, too, has been halted in five of 21 African countries.[12]

The struggle against this campaign is even harder to bring to the surface via the usual statistical methods involving 'conflict' indicators like 'hours lost in strikes'. This is a period when the most important information is micro-social, hence the WB's interest in 'grassroots' studies in Africa. It can be shown, however, that the famines of the 1980s in Africa have not been the result of natural catastrophe, shared evenly by all in the affected area. Rather, they are a consequence of the policies introduced by SAPs, which make famine and war in sub-Saharan Africa more likely; since the promotion of export crops reduces the use of land for food production and raises the prices of even the locally produced foodstuff. A good example of this is to be found in Somalia, where the first SAP agreement between the Somali government and the IMF was signed in 1981. This agreement brought about the liberalization of the economy and an increase in investment in the export crop industry in bananas. The result was the increase of exports in bananas, and a flow of land and investment in capital to that industry with a concomitant reduction of investment in food cropping. The SAP helped motivate an industry where 75 per cent of the profits were shipped abroad and the wages paid to a labour force made up largely of children were below subsistence (Samatar 1993). Such a model, by restricting the best land for export crops and offering below-subsistence wages, is a perfect stimulant for famine and civil war.

It is frequently forgotten that 'successful' capitalist development has often been based upon famine, plague and war, even outside the Americas. The experience of Ireland and the famine of 1846–7, for example, should also be considered as an example of a 'successful' demographic transition and as much a model for 'success' as East Asia in the 1970s. Indeed, the experience of a famine-led demographic transition in Ireland and in the Scottish Highlands increasingly appears to be the model of 'transition' envisaged by the WB for Africa. (Unfortunately, the study of a work like Joel Mokyr's *Why Ireland*

Starved should be required reading for any student of the IMF/WB policies in contemporary Africa (Mokyr 1983).) The vast emigration movement (within Africa and to Europe, the Middle East and North America) set off by the debt crisis is further evidence of the essential similarity between the Irish and Scottish 'transition' and that in Africa today. As the Irish displaced by the 1846 famine ended up in the streets of New York, so too Sudanese and Ethiopians are finding their way to these same streets, a century and a half later, expelled by the same forces.

The debt crisis is affecting today not only the body but also the imagination of Africans, most especially their expectations for the future. Debt is a temporal mechanism; thus the debt crisis has more deleterious consequences than those produced by an 'unequal exchange', for indebtedness jeopardizes the future. The shared recognition that debt has become self-generative tells each prospective African parent that having more children does not bring them closer to appropriating the delayed fruits of independence, but is a human sacrifice to the Moloch of the IMF/WB, bringing a harvest of bullets, tears and diseases.

A major role in the destruction of expectations for the future has been played by the AIDS scare. We can wonder whether the concomitant appearance of the debt crisis and the 'AIDS pandemic' in Central and East Africa was fortuitous. If it was, it has not remained so. The claim that Africa is the origin of AIDS was promoted by the international agencies, including the WB, but this claim has made possible a terrible reality. For this myth has legitimized (unpublicized) large-scale medical experiments on AIDS vaccines in Zaïre and other African countries under the assumption that the subjects were 'high risk', but this experimentation can be AIDS-genic in itself.[13] It has also contributed to devaluing African labour in the diaspora by instigating new curbs on immigration from Africa to Europe and North America, and justifying discrimination against the use of African blood in European and North American blood banks. Finally, the WB and its health and family planning partners (WHO, International Planned Parenthood) have emphasized the transmission of AIDS through sexual (especially extra-marital) intercourse at the expense of other obvious sources of AIDS (contaminated blood supplies provided by European firms and sexual intercourse with European and American troops stationed in Africa and African visitors to Europe and North America). The main anti-AIDS measures and propaganda have accentuated the dangers of having multiple sexual partners and promoted the use of condoms, rather than investing in the treatment of AIDS and the prevention of its spread by medical practice (for example, by distributing free hypodermic needles).

Finally, the debt crisis has undermined the efforts to curtail female genital mutilation and other causes of sterility afflicting African women. The campaign against genital mutilation has been on the agenda of African women since the late 1970s, but in the policies of both the international health agencies (such as WHO) and African governments its elimination is now being relegated to the realm of utopia. Forty per cent of African women have been subjected to clitoridectomy, excision, pharaonic circumcision, and infibulation, and the practice is far from dying out (although its ritual accoutrements are).[14] Indeed, with the southern expansion of Islam in Africa there is evidence that the incidence of genital mutilation is on the rise.

Why are the facts so little known even when international bankers, WB demographers and CIA agents are continually inspecting the statistics concerning African women's genitals? The indifference of international health agencies such as WHO to genital mutilation has often been justified as a sign of respect for local cultural practices, that is, as a recognition of the relativism of cultural mores. But it is likely that a blind eye is turned because it is known that these practices are a form of 'birth control', and even a cause of sterility, as well as a means of control over women's sexual activity. It is significant that, after reviewing the levels and differentials of sterility in Africa, and detailing the evidence linking female genital mutilation to sterility and other forms of infant and maternal mortality, Larsen concluded that:

[I]t is advisable that attempts to reduce sterility be made in the context of integrated family planning services so that successful efforts to combat infertility do not result in an unexpected increase in population growth (Larsen 1989).

Of Debt, Time and Scenarios for the Future

The pace of the current phase of primitive accumulation of the African proletariat is not determined only by commodity market prices and interest rates set in Chicago, New York or London. There is another force here that is appearing on the streets of African, European and North American cities, as well as in the bush. It speaks of another form of life attempting to define a new reality and another exit from the debt crisis. We see it most clearly in the revolutionary organizations of the South African townships and even in the surprising anti-blood-discrimination demonstrations in New York City during the spring of 1990. Less dramatically, there is a deep and widespread anti-privatization ethos in sub-Saharan Africa that is defining a future different from the scenarios of the WB. The very existence of this potential future is the cause of the malthusian pessimism of those who preach the debt crisis. For African capital's return to profitablity is not the only resolution to the debt crisis, even though some theorists on the Left have concluded as much. This future will not be defined by technocrats, or by experts from multinational corporations and international agencies, or by analysts and critics of capitalist strategy like myself.

My task is not to decide how many children African women should have or to inspect and judge, one more time, their sexual practices or desires. Nor is it for me to judge whether a a pro- or anti-natalist programme is appropriate for African societies. The future of African lands, bodies and sexualities is arising out of a struggle within Africa, especially between African men and women. And let us not forget that in this struggle, the protagonists are not weak, helpless beings. As the laments of the planners attest, the African proletariat has proved more resistant to capitalist relations than any other regional group on the planet. Africans have paid for their resistance in blood, misery and death, but they have also preserved and developed an enormous wealth for us all.

Notes

1. A good example of the commonality of assumptions is to be found in the work of Sender and Smith (1986a and 1986b) and George (1988) on the Left and Whitaker (1988) as well as the ideologues of 'fiscal responsibility' of the *Wall Street Journal* variety (Santow 1986) on the Right.
2. For a discussion of the remarkable series of proletarian insurrections ringing the planet against the austerity regimes of the debt crisis, from Zambia in 1986 through Algeria in 1988 and Venezuela in 1989, to Nigeria and Trinidad in 1990, see *Midnight Notes* (1992).
3. For a discussion of the different models of African 'peasant' behaviour see Barker (1989), Chapter 6.
4. This is not to say that the banks have not 'earned their money' in the 1980s. Thus the IMF transferred over $4 billion out of sub-Saharan Africa between 1984 and 1990. Helleiner points out, for example, that 'In the year ending April 30, 1990, about one half of Africa's countries were, on balance, transferring resources to the IMF' (Helleiner 1992).
5. Marx's classic discussion is in Marx (1936), part VIII. Robert Brenner reintroduced the notion of original accumulation as central to the analysis of capitalist relations in the 1970s (Brenner 1976). For a more recent attempt to develop this notion (as well as to criticize the political use of it in Marxist-Leninist movements) see *Midnight Notes* (1990).

6. For the culmination of much of this work in the post-colonial period see Rodney (1972). The debate about the importance of the original African accumulation for industrialization in Europe and North America continues, but Williams (1944) is still the classic text. For recent discussions of the dialectics of the original accumulation and disaccumulation of the proletariat during and immediately after the slave trade period see Pieterse (1989) and Foner (1988). For an account of the period of original accumulation in the colonial period see the articles in Cordell and Gregory (1987).

7. The original text analysing housework as an essential aspect of capitalist reproduction is Dalla Costa, Mariarosa and James, Selma (1972). Since then there have been many works developing this analysis for social reproduction in the Third World, e.g., Dalla Costa, Giovanna Franca (1989), Dalla Costa, Mariarosa (1974).

8. Information concerning the second African diaspora is only beginning to be published, but for an important analysis of the function of this diaspora for capitalist development in Europe see Golini and Bonifazi (1987).

9. For recent reviews of land tenure in Africa see Lesthaeghe (1989b), Davison (1988a) and Bates (1987). For the specific case of Nigeria, the *Third World Encyclopedia* sums up the land tenure situation in the following way: 'Perhaps the only thing common to all the peoples who inhabit Nigeria is communal ownership of land and the absence of any conception of individual property. Under this system the use of land is granted by the chiefs or elders of the tribe and can be taken from the grantee if he fails to cultivate it. According to customary law, land is inalienable; the sale of land is considered a crime. Freehold land outside this system exists only in the case of large plantations and corporations.' It must be remembered that 'customary law' has power even when officially either the state has seized ownership or there has been a private titlization programme. For example, after the 1978 Land Use Decree, which in effect nationalized all land in Nigeria, the actual land use patterns were not dramatically changed. On the other extreme, Place and Hazell note, 'the Kenyan data show that even in a region where all land has been titled, customary restrictions on land rights still prevail and it is not clear that new rights have been created'(Place and Hazell 1993).

10. For a discussion of 'gentrification' and its relation to the old enclosures in seventeenth- and eighteenth-century England, see G. E. Mingay (1963).

11. For a critique of the demographic transition theory as applied to Africa, see Cordell and Gregory (1987).

12. Calculated from statistics of the WHO and the WB's Social Indicators index.

13. For a new classic in 'white man's' medical hysteria concerning AIDS in Africa see Shoumatoff (1988). For a discussion of AIDS that reveals the plans for transforming the AIDS-in-Africa myth to a reality, see the proceedings of the 1988 conference on AIDS in Africa in Giraldo *et al.* (1988), especially the section on 'Cooperative activities in Africa'. A more sceptical approach to the issues involved can be found in Miller and Rockwell (1988). A definitive

discussion on the myth that AIDS had an African origin can be drawn from Federici (1988a) and Chirimuta and Chirimuta (1987). For an African doctor's perspective on the disease see Agadzi (1989), especially his chapter on 'AIDS politics and public concern', where the standard African belief that AIDS is Euro-American in origin is described.

14. There is now a growing literature on 'genital mutilation' in Africa: for Africa as a whole see Hosken (1982), for Sierra Leone see Koso-Thomas (1987), for Sudan see Lightfoot-Klein (1989) and El Dareer (1982), for Somalia see Abdalla (1982).

Bibliography

Abdalla, Raqiya Haji Dualeh (1982). *Sisters in Affliction: Circumcision and Infibulation of Women in Africa*. London: Zed Books.

Acsadi, G. *et al.* (1990). *Population Growth and Reproduction in Sub-Saharan Africa: a World Bank Symposium*. Washington, DC: World Bank.

Africa Research Bulletin. Monthly. Devon, England.

Agadzi, K. (1990). *AIDS: The African Perspective of the Killer Disease*. Accra: Ghana University Publications.

Agawala, A. N. and Singh, S. P. (eds) (1958). *The Economics of Underdevelopment*. London: Oxford University Press.

Andreski, Stansilav (1989). *Syphilis, Puritanism and Witch Hunts*. New York: St Martin's Press.

Arrighi, G. and Saul, J. S. (1973). *Essays on the Political Economy of Africa*. New York: Monthly Review Press.

Barker, Jonathan (1989). *Rural Communities under Stress: Peasant Farmers and the State in Africa*. Cambridge: Cambridge University Press.

Bates, Robert H. (1987). *Political Economy of Rural Africa*. Berkeley: University of California Press.

Bernstein, H. (1977). 'Notes on capital and peasantry'. In *Review of African Political Economy*, 10, pp. 60–73.

Binswanger, Hans P. and Deininger (1993). 'South African land policy: the legacy of history and current options'. In *World Development*, 21, 9, pp. 1451–75.

Bledsoe, Carolyn and Isiugo-Abanihe, Uche (1989). 'Strategies of child fosterage among Mende grannies in Sierra Leone'. In Lesthaeghe (1989).

Blot, Daniel (1990). 'The demographics of migration'. *The OECD Observer*, 163 (April–May).

Bratton, M. and Hyden, G. (1992). *Governance and Politics in Africa*. Boulder, Colorado and London: Lynne Rienner Publishers.

Brenner, Robert (1976). 'Agrarian class structure and economic development in pre-industrial Europe'. In *Past and Present*, 70.

Caldwell, J. C. (1990). 'The soft underbelly of development: demographic transition in condition of limited economic change'. In *Proceedings of the World Bank Annual Conference on Development Economics*. Washington,

DC: World Bank.

Caldwell, J. C. and Caldwell, P. (1990). 'Cultural forces tending to sustain high fertility'. In Acsadi (1990).

Carter, Gwendolen M. and O'Meara, Patrick (eds) (1985). *African Independence: the First Twenty-Five Years.* Bloomington: Indiana University Press.

Cheru, Fantu (1989). *The Silent Revolution in Africa. Debt, Development and Democracy.* London: Zed Books.

Chirimuta, R. C. and Chirimuta, R. J. (1987). *AIDS, Africa and Racism.* London: Free Association Books.

Claudon, Michael P. (ed.) (1986). *World Debt Crisis: International Lending on Trial.* Cambridge, Mass.: Ballinger Publishing Co.

Clausen, A. W. (1986). *The Development Challenge of the Eighties.* Washington, DC: World Bank.

Cleaver, Harry (1988). 'The uses of an earthquake'. In *Midnight Notes*, 9 (Box 204, Jamaica Plain, Mass. 02130).

Cleaver, Harry (1990). 'The origins of the debt crisis'. In *Midnight Notes. New Enclosures.* Jamaica Plain, Mass.: Midnight Notes Publishers.

Commonsense (1988). 'The protest against the World Bank/IMF meeting in Berlin – an interview'. Edinburgh.

Cordell, Dennis D. and Gregory, Joel W. (1987). *African Population and Capitalism: Historical Perspectives.* Boulder, Colorado: Westview Press.

Creevy, Lycy E. (1986). *Women Farmers in Africa.* Syracuse: Syracuse University Press.

Dalla Costa, Giovanna Franca (1978). *Un lavoro d'amore.* Roma: Edizioni delle donne.

Dalla Costa, Giovanna Franca (1989). *La riproduzione nel sottosviluppo. Lavoro delle donne, famiglia e stato nel Venezuela degli anni '70.* Milano: F. Angeli.

Dalla Costa, Maria Rosa (1974). 'Riproduzione e emigrazione' in Serafini, A. (ed.) (1974).

Dalla Costa, M. (1981). 'Emigrazione, immigrazione e composizione di classe in Italia negli anni '70'. In *Economia e Lavoro*, 4 (October–December).

Dalla Costa, M. and James, S. (1972). *The Power of Women and the Subversion of the Community.* Bristol: Falling Wall Press.

Davison, Jean (1988a). 'Land redistribution in Mozambique and its effects on women's collective production: case studies from Sofala Province'. In Davison (1988b).

Davison, Jean (ed.) (1988b). *Agriculture, Women and Land: the African Experience.* Boulder: Westview Press.

Dinham, B. and Hynes, C. (1984). *Agribusiness in Africa.* Trenton, New Jersey: Africa World Press.

Dooley, Michael P. and Watson, C. Maxwell (1989). 'Reinvigorating the debt strategy'. In *Finance and Development*, September 1989, pp. 8–11.

Economist (1986). 'Nigeria Supplement'. London.

Elbadawi, Ibrahim A. (1992). *World Bank Adjustment Lending and Economic Performance in Sub-Saharan Africa in the 1980s.* Washington, DC: World Bank.

El Dareer, Asma (1982). *Woman, Why Do You Weep? Circumcision and Its Consequences.* London: Zed Books.

Faaland, Just (1987). 'Economic disarray and dependence: the case of the Sudan'. In Havnevik (1987).

Fanon, Frantz (1963). *The Wretched of the Earth.* New York: Grove Weidenfeld.

Federici, Silvia (1988a). 'AIDS in Africa?' In *Downtown.* New York, September.

Federici, Silvia (1988b). 'The great witch hunt of the sixteenth century'. In *The Maine Scholar*, 1.

Federici, Silvia (1992). 'The debt crisis, Africa and the new enclosures'. In *Midnight Notes* (1992) .

Federici, S. and Fortunati, P. (1984). *Il Grande Calibano. Storia del Corpo Sociale Ribelle nella Prima Fase del Capitale.* Milano: Franco Angeli Editore.

Foner, Eric (1988). *Reconstruction: America's Unfinished Revolution 1863–1877.* New York: Harper & Row.

Fortunati, L. (1981). *L'arcano della riproduzione. Casalinghe, prostitute, operai e capitale.* Padova: Marsilio.

Foucault, Michel (1977). *The History of Sexuality.* New York: Viking.

George, Susan (1988). *A Fate Worse Than Debt.* New York: Grove Press.

Giraldo, G. *et al.* (1988). *AIDS and Associated Cancers in Africa.* Basel: Karger.

Golini, Antonio and Bonifazi, Corrado (1987). 'Demographic trends and international migration'. OECD (1987).

Goode, William J. (1970). *World Revolution and Family Patterns.* London: Macmillan (first edition 1963).

Greene, Joshua (1989). 'The debt problem of sub-Saharan Africa'. In *Finance and Development*, June 1989, pp. 9–12.

Havnevik, Kjell J. (1987). *The IMF and the World Bank in Africa.* Uppsala: Scandinavian Institute of African Studies.

Helleiner, G.K. (1992). 'The IMF, the World Bank and Africa's adjustment and external debt problems'. In *World Development*, 20, 6 (June).

Hosken, Fran P. (1982). *The Hosken Report: Genital and Sexual Mutilation of Females* (third revised edition). Lexington, Mass.: Women's International Network News.

Humphreys, Charles and Jaeger, William (1989). 'Africa's adjustment and growth'. In *Finance and Development*, June, pp. 6–8.

Hyden, Goran (1985). 'Urban growth and rural development'. In Carter and O'Meara (1985).

IMF (1989). *World Economic Outlook.* Washington, DC: IMF.

Jackson, Robert H. and Rosberg, Carl G. (1985). 'The marginality of African states'. In Carter and O'Meara (1985).

Kennedy, Paul (1990). *African Capitalism. The Struggle for Ascendancy.* Cambridge: Cambridge University Press (first edition 1988).

Killick, Tony (1980). *Papers on the Kenyan Economy: Performance, Problems and Policies.* Nairobi: Heinemann.

Korner, Peter *et al.* (1986). *The IMF and the Debt Crisis: a Guide to the Third World's Dilemma.* London: Zed Books.

Koso-Thomas, Olayinka (1987). *The Circumcision of Women: A Strategy for Eradication.* London: Zed Books.

Larsen, Ulla (1989). 'A comparative study of the levels and differentials of sterility in Cameroun, Kenya and Sudan'. In Lesthaeghe (1989a).

Lawrence, Peter R. (ed.) (1986). *World Recession and the Food Crisis in Africa.* London: James Currey.

Lesthaeghe, R. J. (ed.) (1989a). *Reproduction and Social Organization in Sub-Saharan Africa.* Berkeley: University of California Press.

Lesthaeghe, R. J. (1989b). 'Production and reproduction in sub-Saharan Africa: an overview of organizing principles'. In Lesthaeghe, R. J. (1989a).

Lesthaeghe, R. J. (1989c). 'Social organization, economic crises, and the future of fertility control in Africa'. In Lesthaeghe (1989a).

Lewis, W. Arthur (1958). 'Economic development with unlimited supplies of labour'. In Agawala and Singh (1958).

Lightfoot-Klein, Hanny (1989). *Prisoners of Ritual: an Odyssey into Female Genital Circumcision in Africa.* New York: Harrington Park Press.

Loxley, John (1987). 'The IMF, the World Bank, and sub-Saharan Africa: policies and politics'. In Havnevik (1987).

Marx, Karl (1936). *Capital: a Critique of Political Economy.* New York: Modern Library.

Midnight Notes (1990). *The New Enclosures.* New York: Autonomedia.

Midnight Notes (eds) (1992). *Midnight Oil. Work, Energy, War. 1973–1992.* New York: Autonomedia.

Mies, Maria (1986). *Patriarchy and Accumulation on a World Scale.* London: Zed Books.

Miller, Norman and Rockwell, Richard C. (eds) (1988). *AIDS in Africa: the Social and Policy Impact.* Lewiston/Queenston: The Edwin Mellen Press.

Mingay, G. E. (1963). *Landed Society in the Eighteenth Century.* London: Routledge and Kegan Paul.

Mokyr, Joel (1983). *Why Ireland Starved: a Quantitative and Analytic History of the Irish Economy 1800–1850.* London: George Allen and Unwin.

O'Brien, Jay (1986). 'Sowing the seeds of famine: the political economy of food deficits in Sudan'. In Lawrence (1986).

Okoth-Ogendo, H. W. O. (1980). 'Land ownership and land distribution in Kenya's large-farm areas'. In Killick (1980).

OECD (1987). *The Future of Migration.* Paris: OECD Publications.

Page, Hilary (1989). 'Childrearing versus childbearing: coresidence of mother and child in sub-Saharan Africa'. In Lesthaeghe (1989).

Pankhurst, Donna and Jacobs, Susie (1988). 'Land tenure, gender relations and agricultural production: the case of Zimbabwe's peasantry'. In Davison (1988).

Payer, Cheryl (1982). *The World Bank.* New York: Monthly Review Press.

Pieterse, Jan Nederveen (1989). *Empire and Emancipation: Power and Liberation on a World Scale.* New York: Praeger.

Place, Frank and Hazell, Peter (1993). 'Productivity effects of indigenous land tenure systems in sub-Saharan Africa'. *American Journal of Agricultural*

Economics, 75, pp. 10–19.

Rau, Bill (1992). *From Feast to Famine. Official Cures and Grassroots Remedies to Africa's Food Crisis*. London: Zed Books.

Ravenhill, John (ed.) (1986). *Africa in Economic Crisis*. New York: Columbia University Press.

Reyna, S. P. (1987). 'The emergence of land concentration in the West African savanna'. In *American Ethnologist*, 14, 3, pp. 523–41.

Rodney, W. (1972). *How Europe Underdeveloped Africa*. Dar es Salaam and London: Tanzania Publishing House and Bogle-L'Ouverture Publications.

Sachs, Wolfgang (1992). *The Development Dictionary: A Guide to Knowledge as Power*. London: Zed Books.

Samatar, Abdi Ismail (1993). 'Structural adjustment as developmental strategy: bananas, boom and poverty in Somalia'. *Economic Geography*, 69, 1, pp. 25–43.

Santow, Leonard J. (1986). 'The view From Wall Street'. In Claudon (1986).

Schoepf, Brooke Grundfest (1986). 'Food crisis and class formation in Zaire: political ecology in Shaba'. In Lawrence (1986).

Schoepf, Brooke Grundfest and Schoepf, Claude (1988). 'Land, gender and food security in Eastern Kivu, Zaire'. In Davison (1988).

Sender, John and Smith, Sheila (1986a). 'What's right with the Berg Report and what's left of its criticisms'. In Lawrence (1986).

Sender, John and Smith, Sheila (1986b). *The Development of Capitalism in Africa*. London: Methuen.

Serafini, A. (1974). *L'operaio multinazionale in Europa*. Milano: Feltrinelli.

Shoumatoff, Alex (1988). *African Madness*. New York: A. Knopf.

Summers, Lawrence H. and Pritchett, Lant H. (1993). 'The structural adjustment debate'. In *American Economic Review*, 83, 2, pp. 383–9.

Timberlake, Lloyd (1986). *Africa in Crisis*. Philadelphia: Earthscan Publications.

Toyo, Eskor (1986). 'Food and hunger in a petroleum neo-colony: a study of the food crisis in Nigeria'. In Lawrence (1986).

US Bureau of the Census (1989), *World Population Profile*. Washington, DC: US Government Printing Office.

Wall Street Journal (1986). 'What Africa Doesn't Need'. 22 September.

Whitaker, Jennifer Seymour (1988). *How Can Africa Survive?* New York: Council on Foreign Relations Press.

Williams, Eric (1944). *Capitalism and Slavery*. Durham: University of North Carolina Press.

Wisner, Ben (1989). *Power and Need in Africa*. Trenton, NJ: Africa World Press.

World Bank (1981). *Accelerated Development in sub-Saharan Africa*. Washington, DC: World Bank.

World Bank (1989a). *Sub-Saharan Africa: from Crisis to Sustainable Growth. A Long-term Perspective*. Washington, DC: World Bank.

World Bank (1989b). *World Development Report*. Oxford: Oxford University Press.

World Bank (1991). *World Debt Tables*. Washington, DC: World Bank.

Zerowork (1975). 'Introduction', Vol. 1. New York.

3

ECONOMIC CRISIS AND DEMOGRAPHIC POLICY IN SUB-SAHARAN AFRICA
The Case of Nigeria

Silvia Federici

It is commonly acknowledged, in the current demographic studies, that the 1980s have registered a significant change in the demographic thinking of African policy makers. For in this decade most African governments, reversing a historic pro-natalist trend, have made family planning and birth control a key component, if not a priority, of their social programmes.

The new demographic course, first endorsed by the Organization of African Unity (OAU) at the Arusha Conference of 1984, has generated many speculations concerning the factors that may have inspired it and its likely prospects. Concerning its reasons, the most accredited theory maintains that the new course resulted from the lesson which the African governments learnt during the 1970s, when presumably it became evident that the economic development of the region would not lead to a reduction, but to an increase, in fertility rates. As a prominent advocate of this position has argued:

> it was realized that African societies have always had a marked pattern of child-spacing implemented through prolonged breastfeeding and post-partum abstinence, and that this long-standing tradition was being eroded rather than supported by increased education, rising income, and especially urbanization. Without a countervailing force capable of restoring the older patterns of child-spacing, it was feared that such a change could lead to a deterioration of maternal and child health, to a slowing down of the infant mortality decline, and possibly to a fertility bulge. It was clear, at least during an initial phase, that socio-economic development was not automatically 'the best contraceptive'. From that point onward, forms of fertility regulation were much harder to categorize as Western inventions, and contraception achieved legitimation as a necessary corrective for the declining authentically African pattern of child-spacing (Lesthaeghe 1989: 475).

Lesthaeghe considers as additional factors motivating the new demographic course a succession of pan-African 'ecological, agricultural and political crises' (Lesthaeghe 1989: 475–6). But his account remains focused on the *exceptionality* of Africa's demographic response to development. As I will argue, however, this theory cannot be accepted. For even assuming that the economic boom which several African countries experienced in the 1970s can be qualified as 'development', and there are good reasons not to do so, it cannot be imagined that African policy makers would have taken such an unprecedented step and embarked on a demographic *perestroika* on the basis of only one decade of developmental experience; as an outstanding historical record exists demonstrating that 'demographic changes are slow and produce effects – often intangible – only in the … very long term' (Golini and Bonifazi 1987: 110). This theory appears even more untenable if we consider that rarely in the 1970s, even under the best economic circumstances, have African governments provided the social services and conditions (access to education, health care, security with respect to employment and to the future) that at the First World Population Conference, held in Bucharest in 1974, were identified and recommended as preconditions for a 'demographic transition' (Salas 1985). Most important, we should not lose sight of the fact that in capitalist economies, even in conditions of 'underdevelopment', the 'optimal size of the population' is not assessed on the basis of purely quantitative criteria, but is determined by 'quality' considerations, such as the productivity of those who must be reproduced (Dalla Costa 1974). On the basis of these premises, our first thesis is that the so-called 'population crisis' in Africa is in fact a political crisis and a crisis of profitability. That is, Africa's demographic growth is a cause of concern because the African population is not considered sufficiently productive to provide incentives to capital investment; consequently its 'unchecked' growth is perceived as a threat to the economic and political 'stability' of the region. In other words, the 'demographic crisis' should be seen above all as a result of both the profit crisis that has characterized much of sub-Saharan Africa in the 1970s and 1980s, and the decision by national and international capital not to invest in the region until an environment is created more favourable to business: an environment, that is, where the cost of labour is reduced and so is the quota of public spending devoted to social consumption. These, in fact, have been the main objectives of the Structural Adjustment Programmes (SAPs) which, since 1985, the World Bank and the International Monetary Fund (IMF) have imposed on more than thirty African governments as a condition for economic recovery.

This assessment of the reasons for the new demographic course in Africa leads us to an evaluation of its prospects that precludes any optimism. We believe, in fact, that the new demographic policy adopted by African governments cannot have positive results. In the first place, it is built upon an erroneous correlation between poverty and demographic growth; in the second, far from being inspired by the wish to raise the standard of living of the population, it is a product of a policy of economic retrenchment which has already had devastating consequences for the lives of the African people. Nor is there any light at the end of the tunnel. For, if our hypothesis is correct, then the present economic retrenchment is part of a strategy adopted by the African governments, under the guidance of the World Bank and the IMF, in order to reduce the cost of labour and thus make African labour more competitive on the international market. However, in a climate of growing competition among workers all over the world, this spells a regime of stiff austerity for many years to come, with no guarantee that African workers will ever manage to obtain income levels enabling them even to survive.

This pessimistic appraisal of the new demographic course in Africa is well supported by the experience of Nigeria where, in its cumulative impact, the SAP is already functioning as a means of population control. It is also justified by the fact that the inevitability of a classically malthusian, 'crisis-led' 'demographic transition' is increasingly being theorized in the most influential circles of demographic planning (Lesthaeghe 1989: 475–6).

The case of Nigeria is especially significant because its demographic plan, adopted in 1989, has been considered one of the most progressive in the region. For the National Population Policy (NPP) not only pledges the government's support for family planning, but confirms the government's commitment to the promotion of health care, public education and the improvement of the status of women. Thus, at its face value, the NPP would appear as a model of enlightened social policy and respect for human rights. However, there is no evidence that the promises made by the NPP will ever materialize, as they are contradicted, point by point, by the economic policy the Nigerian government has pursued since the adoption of the SAP, which cuts social spending in the very sectors – health, education, nutrition – that are considered crucial to a 'demographic transition'. In reality, the only population policy at work now in Nigeria is a malthusian one, which relies on the classic positive checks: hunger, illness, violent death, migration. Thus Nigeria is a prime example of how the economic crisis and the SAPs are *de facto* operating in Africa as means of demographic control.

The Nigerian Case

The demographic experience of Nigeria invalidates the theory according to which the concern with population growth proceeded in sub-Saharan Africa from the realization that development has no positive impact on 'fertility rates'. As has often been pointed out, throughout the 1970s, Nigeria's population growth rates were considered satisfactory by the country's rulers and economists. Policy makers at the time were fond of stressing that historically an abundant supply of labour has proved to be an incentive to economic development. Fears about demographic growth emerged only in the early 1980s, in an economic context marked by the outflow of foreign investments and rising complaints concerning business unprofitability and the indiscipline of the Nigerian workforce. By the end of the 1970s the profit rate in manufacturing industry had been falling quite dramatically – from 43 per cent in 1975 to 19 per cent in 1978 (Abba *et al.* 1985) – while workers' protests kept escalating. Then, in 1979

> in the first nine months of the Second Republic ... the country recorded 247 officially registered trade disputes involving 144, 886 workers, leading to the loss of over one million work-days. This did not include the hundreds of sporadic, short-lived and wild-cat strikes. In 1980, the country recorded a loss of 2,551,000 work-days involving 220,988 workers in 416 registered strike actions (Falola and Ihonvbere 1985: 154).

This was followed in 1981 by a two-day general strike (Otobo 1981) which, coinciding with a glut on the world oil market, prompted President Shehu Shagari to predict that :

> With the glut in the oil market and with the concomitant decline in oil prices, workers' demands on the economy are likely to generate more crises, not less. (Falola and Ihonvbere 1985: 155).

By 1984 the new government of General Buhari, which took power in an end-of-the-year military coup, was beginning to negotiate with the IMF for the rescheduling of payments on Nigeria's external debt, calculated at the time as $20 billion. It had also officially endorsed a restrictive economic policy that within months was to lead to the retrenchment of 30 per cent of workers in the public sector and to a wage freeze.

The 'population threat' then escalated in proportion to the steady decline of the oil revenues through 1985 and 1986, when warnings against the impending 'population explosion' began to merge with the 'party is over' rhetoric, which suggested that Nigerians had excessively profited from the 'oil boom' and now had to pay back. Thus, already under the regime of General Buhari (1984–5) population control became the official government policy, and forces were mobilized to instruct the country on the virtues of reduced family size. Army officers started distributing contraceptives among their ranks, reminding the soldiers that 'virility' does not hang on the number of children one has, while 'unrestrained procreation' was labelled unpatriotic and made a target of the new War Against Indiscipline (WAI).

In the aftermath of the General I. Babangida coup of August 1985, as the negotiations between the new military regime, the IMF and the World Bank intensified, leading to the adoption of an SAP in 1986, so did the campaign in favour of population control. Articles discussing the relation between population and development flooded the media, seminars on the consequences of the 'population explosion' were organized all over the country, employers were urged to promote family planning and birth control in the workplace. Meanwhile, foreign experts were given the green light for a wide range of activities: con-ducting demographic surveys, running workshops on birth control, building surgical theatres to demonstrate the technique of vasectomy. These initiatives were not only supported but often financed by the World Bank and its sister agencies: IDA (International Development Agency), USAID (US Agency for International Development) and UNFPA (United Nations Fund for Population Activities). USAID provided millions of units of birth control pills, UNFPA helped to coordinate the first national family planning programme, and the World Bank loaned millions of dollars to facilitate the spread of family planning among the rural population. The World Bank also provided the ideological framework in which the 'population threat' was conceptualized, reiterating what over the years has become its approach to the problems of the 'Third World'. Far from acknowledging the impact of international interest rates, falling commodity prices, and government mismanagment of funds as key factors in the Nigerian 'debt crisis', the Bank identified demographic growth as the primary cause behind the economic ills of the country, warning, in various annual reports, that it would inevitably reduce human-capital invest-ment *per capita*, expand the number of young 'economically inactive people' and slow down capital formation (Clausen 1986).

According to the World Bank, with its 3.3 per cent population growth rate Nigeria was already outpacing its resources and preparing for an economic and ecological catastrophe. Nigerians learned that population growth was outpacing food growth in the ratio of 3 to 1, and short of reducing their birth rates they would soon be confronted with shortages of food, housing, fuel, teachers and with a steadily deteriorating environment. Such forecasts were well publicized by the government authorities, who were facing the problem of having to impose stiff austerity measures on a population that was still waiting to see the benefits of the wealth the country had acquired during the oil boom. Thus, commenting on the prospect of a population that would double in the coming 22 years, Health Minister Ransome-Kuti warned that

> this would have dire consequences for the country … at a time when its national income is declining, [for] the resulting inability of the government to provide social services, food and work can be a great source of discontent. Revolutions have been provoked by situations of this nature and no government can allow it to happen (*Nigerian Guardian* 28 November 1985).

But despite an intensive propaganda campaign, it soon became clear that a population control policy would be highly controversial, and the NPP was long in the offing. Moreover, when it was approved, it disappointed those who had asked for more stringent measures: taxing women who procreated beyond the optimal number, for example, or adopting 'one man one wife' or 'one couple one child' policies.

The government at first had seemed inclined to set guidelines establishing the proper family size, and to enforce them by means of disincentives. Thus, in February 1986, the Health Ministry had announced that it had drafted a proposal to offer disincentives to couples against having more than four children (*Guardian* 18 February 1986). The proposal called for the withdrawal of maternity leave for women who had more than four children, and the raising of the age of marriage. But the National Population Policy eventually adopted made it clear that while the goverment would promote family planning, population control would remain a matter of individual choice (United Nations Department of Internal Economic and Social Affairs 1988: 24–5). This was well advised. One must 'only' consider the role that demographic numbers play in the allocation of economic revenues, the fear that Nigerians have of ethnic discrimination, and the different demographic possibilities of monogamous versus polygamous families, in order to realize that mandatory measures would have been strongly resisted. Moreover, the population debate that the government initiative spurred showed that the opposition to population control was widespread in many quarters. Conservatives (religious leaders, traditional rulers) objected to it on religious and moral grounds, depicting family planning as an incentive to 'sexual laxity' and an attack on male prerogatives in the family. The Left criticized it as a diversion from the real economic and political issue, namely the unequal distribution of economic wealth and power. Others pointed to the involvement of Western-dominated, multinational agencies in the campaign for population control as a proof that the 'population scare' was a capitulation to Western interests, if not a ploy by the white man to further plunder the continent of its resources. Given the legacy of colonial rule, Nigerians are legitimately suspicious of the interest Western donors and agencies have taken in the reorganization of their demographic life. People noticed, for instance, that not only the rhetoric but also the logistic and financial infra-structures of family planning were imported from Europe and the US, with dozens of foreign organizations active in the field. Columbia University trained market women as birth control agents, Johns Hopkins conducted courses on the impact of population growth, New York University provided surgical contraception services at the University of Benin. 'Why is it – many asked – that the rich and most powerful nations are showing such profound interest in limiting the birth rates of our people?' and 'why is it they consider themselves best equipped in prescribing remedies for our problems?' (*Daily Times* 7 November 1985). Could it be, some suggested, that the fear about increasing numbers of African children is due to the fact that much wealth is to be gained from the exploitation of African labour, but 'if the teaming masses have no food, no houses, no employment they may rise up?' (Heinecke 1986: 52).

Most importantly, the government campaign has failed to convince the majority of Nigerians that poverty is the result of population growth, and that a reduction of 'fertility rates' would bring prosperity to them. In this case, too, there are legitimate reasons for such scepticism. For the argument that population growth is the cause of poverty clashes with the realization that families have many children because children are considered an asset, as they provide labour and income to the family and are a guarantee against old age and disease in a country where the most basic forms of social security are missing. This was acknowledged by the *World Development Report* of 1984 (World Bank 1984: 69) which, however, concluded that here we have a classic example of how private interest can run counter to the public good. For there are presumably 'externalities' to be considered in evaluating how generally advantageous the decision of people to have children might be. Such 'externalities' include the impact of procreation both on public assets, such as land or minerals, and on public services (Lee and Miller 1990). But the assumption on which such considerations are based is that people actually have the control and use of public assets. In Nigeria, however, this has hardly been the case. Only a minimal part of the oil wealth accumulated in the 1970s has been devoted to improving the standard of living of the population, while the bulk has been spent to provide an infrastructure for business operations, or to finance projects that have served the needs of only a small élite, when it has not been embezzled or illegally exported.

Not only has economic planning in Nigeria – through successive regimes – been notorious for its mismanagement of the national wealth (Falola and Ihonvbere 1985). Nigerians have also witnessed the squandering of their resources by foreign investors. For instance, while millions of Nigerians have no electricity in their homes and the government has had to import crude gas, for decades, practically since the beginning of the oil extraction in the 1950s, the oil companies have flared the natural gas, because they have not found it profitable to process it (Abba *et al.*. 1985: 83–5). As the *Financial Times* reported (12 March 1991), according to some estimates, a volume of natural gas six times larger than the one consumed in the country, and with a potential value of 4 billion dollars, is flared every year. The oil companies have also been responsible for the loss of large tracts of arable land, and the pollution of fishing grounds and water supplies, through petroleum spills and reckless drilling practices – all phenomena which have had a negative impact on the ability of Nigerians to feed themselves (Saro-Wiwa 1992). Indeed, a study of the impact of business operations on the standard of living of the majority of Nigerians would have to conclude that the present population scare is a classic case of 'blaming the victim'.

There is evidence, moreover, that the widening gap between the growth of food supplies and population growth is the result of the development plans of the 1970s that, by concentrating investments in the oil sector, undermined agriculture and provided incentives for land privatization and urbanization. The Agricultural Development Projects (ADP) which the World Bank has sponsored have contributed to the spreading of hunger in the rural and urban areas. The expansion of export-oriented, capital-intensive farming has expropriated the land of many farmers who drew from it their subsistence, and who subsequently were rarely able to acquire an income sufficient to purchase the food they no longer produced, now made ever more expensive by the export policy. Yet boosting the export of agricultural products remains a top priority for the the World Bank's SAP. Thus, Nigeria may soon experience the situation which the World Bank in its 1986 *Report on Hunger and Poverty in the World* noted as a general condition of Third World countries: while food supplies world-wide have grown faster than population, most people in the Third World still go hungry because they don't have enough money to buy food.

High 'Fertility Rates' as a Rationalization

Demographic surveys have demonstrated that the high 'fertility rates' that characterize demographic behaviour in Nigeria are not due to people's ignorance of contraceptive methods, nor are they a sign of blind attachment to traditional customs. As a demographic study conducted in the South-Western region of Nigerian in the period 1970–5 indicates, Nigerians do practise birth control, and have a conception of what the 'ideal family' size should be, which varies depending on their economic situation (Farooq 1985: 312). Thus if they have many children it is because they wish to have them, and consider it advantageous to do so, rather than because they are poorly informed concerning contraceptive techniques, or do not understand what are the consequences of a large family.

Nigerian demographic patterns are best understood through the framework developed by Gregory and Piche (1981), who claim that Africa's high 'fertility rates' are a 'survival strategy' or 'defence mechanism' adopted by people to enable them to cope with the conditions created by underdevelopment. African families, they argue, have a large number of children because they must reproduce workers both for the waged sector and for the unwaged sectors; for in underdevelopment the family cannot manage to survive either exclusively on the basis of a wage, or exclusively on the basis of subsistence farming. As Gregory and Piche conclude, a case can be made that with lower 'fertility rates' people would be poorer and more defenceless against old age, disease and the state:

> Some studies of African population see the present demographic system as a contradiction in the face of expanding capitalism, as a vestige of an earlier 'primitive' state. Demographic behaviour, and high fertility in particular, is also seen as an obstacle to development. We assert that, on the contrary, the household unit of production and reproduction has adapted to the necessities of peripheral capitalist development, with high fertility and substantial mobility providing the only means of survival. High fertility, far from being an obstacle to development, is a continuing response to underdevelopment (Gregory and Piche 1981: 29–30).

The rationality for high fertility in a situation of underdevelopment should be understood as a survival strategy. Lowering fertility would jeopardize domestic production (and reproduction of the domestic economy). Domestic production is essential for the survival of household members; of

those who are salaried but earn just enough for their day-to-day maintenance, and of those who are, or will become, unproductive. Under present
conditions of underdevelopment, the end result of lower fertility would
probably be greater impoverishment, famine, and perhaps even increased
morbidity and mortality (Gregory and Piche 1981: 28).

We cannot sufficiently stress that women and children have paid the
highest cost for this survival strategy – a cost which is reflected in the
high mortality and infirmity rates to which women are subject, due to
childbirth-related complications, chronic debilitation and overwork.
Every year in Nigeria 70,000 women die of childbirth-related complications, more than 140 a day, the equivalent of a daily plane crash (*African
Concord* 24 July 1989). Moreover, the position of women in the family
and society has been negatively affected by the need to procreate, as
women are constantly in danger of being ostracized by their husbands
and in-laws should they fail to procreate an adequate number of
children or a male offspring. From this point of view, women are the
ideal constituency for the government family planning campaign, and
it is plausible that a social policy genuinely aimed at improving their
conditions – that is, at ensuring their economic autonomy within the
family and therefore their ability 'to choose' – would have generated a
different type of debate, and gone a long way in the direction of a
'demographic transition'. But all the declarations that have been made
on the need to improve the status of women have been *de facto* belied
by the steady deterioration of women's economic position in the wake
of the implementation of the SAP.

It is precisely when we confront it with the situation of women that
we see more clearly the vacuousness of the NPP. Only economic
independence from husbands and relatives would enable Nigerian
women to decide how many children they wish to have, and under what
conditions. But in the context of the SAP this remains a utopia. In fact,
the condition of women in Nigeria has constantly deteriorated over the
last five years and today is worse than ever. Traditionally the poorest
among the poor, women have been those most severely affected by the
economic crisis and the restructuring of production and commerce
which has followed the implementation of the SAP. They have been the
first to be retrenched in the private and the public sector; and their main
source of income, trading, has come under government attack through
the imposition of fees, the introduction of zoning regulations and the
trend towards government-controlled supermarkets. Women have also
been displaced as farmers, because of the expansion of export-oriented
agriculture which, being more mechanized, has favoured the employment of men (WIN 1985a). Women are also losing ground with respect

to education, as parents do not believe that their daughters have any-thing to gain by acquiring a diploma when so many young men are unemployed. In the 1980s, some states (Niger State, for example) have enacted edicts restraining parents from taking their daughters out of school in order to marry them off. But in the absence of any alternatives, such measures have remained ineffective. Thus, the vicious circle of poverty and early marriage continues. The educational prospects of Nigerian women at present are summed up in the words of Lesthaeghe, Kaufmann and Meekers:

> The current economic crisis in sub-Saharan Africa is also of relevance for the future of ages at marriage and polygyny. The formal sectors of the economy are no longer growing at rates comparable with those in the decades following independence and the demand for better educated labor often trails far behind the supply. The returns from investing in children's education are falling and school systems are under considerable strain for both financial and demographic reasons. Hence the current economic crisis is not propitious for the enhancement of female education and a continuation of the female nuptiality transition (Lesthaeghe *et al* 1989: 329).

The contradiction between what the NPP promises to women and the realities of the SAP is most evident in the health care field, especially with regard to the health services that are more directly relevant to family planning. Should women today wish to practise birth control, they would find it difficult unless they had access to a Planned Parent-hood Centre. For it is one of the requirements of the SAP that health-care must be 'cost-effective'. This means that women, whose incomes have fallen to the lowest levels, must now pay dearly for medical services that previously were free, for most pharmaceutical products have to be imported and repeated devaluations of the naira have made import prices skyrocket. Meanwhile, even a trip to the nearest clinic, often located many miles away, has become a costly affair, due to the tripling of the cost of public transport, following the withdrawal of state sub-sidies from domestically sold petroleum.

In this context, not only does the implementation of the SAP belie the promises of the NPP, and the official rhetoric concerning the need to improve the status of women, but it is itself becoming a substitute means of demographic control.

Structural Adjustment as an Instrument of Population Control

When it was adopted in 1986 the SAP was presented by the Babangida government as an indigenous product. In reality the programme is similar to the dozens others that have been imposed by the IMF and the World Bank on indebted Third World countries in the 1980s. It contains all the standard features to be found in any of these programmes from Nigeria to Bangladesh: the devaluation of the local currency (the value of the naira has fallen by 97 per cent since 1985); the 'rationalization' of the public sector (which has led to an almost 50 per cent cut in public sector employment); the reduction of subsidies to food and fuel (a 50 per cent increase in the price of domestically sold petrol); the introduction of 'user fees' for all public services, such as education and health (fees have also been reintroduced in primary schools); the privatization of state-owned and parastatal industries; the liberalization of trade and the restructuring of production on an export-oriented basis.

These drastic measures, which have affected prices, wages and unemployment rates, have yet failed to produce the promised economic recovery. So far they have not stimulated the growth rate or capital formation, which fell from 20 per cent of GDP in the early 1980s to 15 per cent in 1989. Nor have they increased the capacity utilization in manufacturing (which still remained below 50 per cent in 1989); nor have they 'resurrected private investment'. Thus, as an economic growth policy, SAP has definitively been a failure. But as a demographic policy it has had an impact on some of the most important malthusian indicators :

	1960	1970	1975	1981	1989
Crude birth rate (per 1000)	52	50	50	49	46
Crude death rate (per 1000)	25	21	19	17	17
Life expectancy	39	44	46	49	48

(*Source*: US Bureau of the Census, *World Population Profile: 1989* and World Bank, *World Social Indicators*, 1984)

For the first time in the post-colonial period life expectancy has fallen, the death rate has stagnated and the birth rate has fallen steeply. If we combine these statistics with the fact that infant mortality has fallen from 133 (per 1000) in 1981 to 121 in 1989, we must conclude that there has been a substantial increase in non-infant mortality, undoubtedly correlated with the introduction of the SAP, that has caused an increase in malnutrition and morbidity, in addition to determining a migratory wave whose dimension probably rivals, in relative terms, the diaspora induced by the slave trade.

There is hardly an aspect of the SAP that does not affect demographic rates. As we have seen, SAP has meant the cutting back, and often the elimination, of many social programmes and subsidies (to food, to locally consumed petroleum, to health and education), the freezing of wages, a manifold increase in the prices of all commodities, massive unemployment. All of these factors are particularly devastating in their cumulative impact. Health care, for instance, has not been affected only by the privatization of medical services and reduced government spending (in 1990 only a meagre 1.5 per cent of the federal budget was reserved to it). It is also affected by transport costs, the higher costs of drugs and hospital prices, and the diaspora of medical and paramedical personnel over the last few years. Hundreds of doctors and nurses have left the country, demoralized by the collapse of the medical infrastructures and the fall of their own standard of living. This is happening in a country where even prior to the introduction of the SAP patients faced an average waiting period of eight hours before being able to see a doctor (World Bank 1988), and where infant mortality was one of the highest in the world. The consequences of the dismantling of the health care services can be measured by the recrudescence of epidemics in recent years. Cholera, yellow fever and meningitis have long been present in Nigeria, with chronic seasonal outbursts, but recently they have assumed unprecedented proportions. According to the *African Concord* of 6 May 1991:

> In less than a year, more than 3,000 deaths have resulted from the attack of such diseases as cholera, cerebro-spinal meningitis and gastroenteritis. The poor state of the healthcare system ... appears to be a strong factor responsible for the high death rate. Last September in under three weeks, more than 100 people died from gastroenteritis attacks in Jezawa and Ringini local government areas. According to an alarmed health official, 'we have never witnessed any strange disease of this sort before'. (p. 33)

A crucial element in the impact of the SAP on the lives of the Nigerians is the collapse of *per capita* income. According to World Bank estimates, this has fallen from $800 in the early 1980s to about $370 in 1987 (*West Africa* 8 January 1988), while in the meantime prices have kept rising, including the prices of locally produced foodstuffs, which have become scarce due to the export policy, and more costly to transport following the cuts in petroleum subsidies. In 1988 alone the price of food rose by 44 per cent (*FET* June 1989: 9). Thus even in the South-Western region, traditionally the yam basket of Africa, hunger and malnutrition are widespread. Even among the middle class meat is becoming a luxury, while for the majority of the population the daily meal consists of nothing more than a bowl of *gari*, the least nutritious of all staples though its price has increased five times over the last four years.

The despair the SAP has caused among Nigerians can be measured by the increase in the number of suicides, new illnesses (hypertension and mental illness, for example) and crime. Prisons are overcrowded, and there, too, the mortality rate is very high, since the convicts are generally left without medical assistance and often without food. According to the Nigerian Civil Liberty Organization (CLO) the death rate at the maximum security prison of Kirikiri (Lagos) now stands at 3 inmates per week (*African Guardian* 9 April 1990).

In this situation many have been forced to emigrate. Indeed the most revealing image of the consequences of the SAP in the 1980s has been that of the foreign embassies besieged by thousands of people whose only hope was to leave their homes and their country.

Viewed in this context, the campaign of the Nigerian government to create incentives for family planning seems above all to be ideological in character, and it is foreseeable that as long as the present economic policies prevail the SAP will remain Nigeria's only population policy. As we have seen, the objective of the SAP is to make Nigeria competitive on the international labour market, so as to attract foreign investment and reactivate the process of economic development. This implies that Nigerian workers have to 'compete' with the workers of all the Third World – now integrated into the circuit of international capital from India to China and Russia – on whom the World Bank and the IMF are presently imposing the same programmes of 'economic recovery'.

It is therefore legitimate to conclude that the great impoverishment that can be seen today in Nigeria, as in much of the Third World, is destined to last for an indefinite time, and that the so-called 'demographic transition', rather than being led by an improvement in the conditions of life of the people, will rely instead on the classic malthusian checks – poverty, war and disease. This, at least, is the likely outcome as long as the survival of the Nigerian population continues to be conditioned by its utility for the development of international capital.

Bibliography

Abba, A. *et al.* (1985). *The Nigerian Economic Crisis: Causes and Solutions.* Zaria: Academic Staff Union of Universities of Nigeria.
Africa Research Bulletin (1989). 31 May.
African Concord (1989). 24 July.
African Concord (1991). 6 May.

African Guardian (1990). 9 April.

Bangura, Y. (1987). 'IMF /World Bank conditionality and Nigeria's structural adjustment program'. In Havnevik (1987).

Bratton, M. (1989). 'Beyond the state: civil society and associational life in Africa'. In *World Politics,* 41, 3 (April 1989), pp. 407–30.

Clausen, A.W. (1986). *The Development Challenge of the Eighties.* Washington, DC: World Bank.

Congressional Budget Office (United States Congress) (1989). *Agricultural Progress in the Third World and Its Effects on US Farm Exports.* Washington, DC: US Government Printing Office.

Dalla Costa, M. (1974). 'Riproduzione e emigrazione'. In Serafini (ed.) (1974).

Daily Times (Nigeria) (1985). 7 November.

Davison, J. (ed.) (1988). *Agriculture, Women, and Land. The African Experience.* London: Westview Press.

Eberstadt, Nick (1986). 'What Africa doesn't need'. *Wall Street Journal,* 22 September 1986.

Entwisle, B. and Coles, C. M. (1990). 'Demographic surveys and Nigerian women'. In *Signs: Journal of Women in Culture and Society,* 15, 2.

Falola, T. and Ihonvbere, J. (1985). *The Rise and Fall of Nigeria's Second Republic.* London: Zed Books.

Fantu, C. (1989). *The Silent Revolution in Africa.* London: Zed Books.

Farooq, G. M. (1985). 'Household fertility decision-making in Nigeria'. In Farooq and Simmons (1985).

Farooq, G. M. and Simmons, G. B. (1985). *Fertility in Developing Countries.* New York: St Martin's Press.

Federici, S. (1992). 'The debt crisis, Africa and the new enclosures'. In *Midnight Oil* (eds), *Midnight Oil. Work, Energy,War 1973–1992.* New York: Autonomedia.

Federici, S. and Ogbuagu, S. (1985). 'Women and work in the urban areas'. In *Women in Nigeria* (1985a).

Foreign Economic Trends (FET) (1989). Washington, DC: US Department of Commerce, June.

Golini, A. and Bonifazi, C. (1987). 'Demographic trends and international migration'. In OECD (1987).

Gregory, J. W. and Piche, V. (1981). *The Demographic Process of Peripheral Capitalism Illustrated with African Examples.* Working Papers Series N. 29. Centre for Developing-Area Studies, McGill University, Montreal.

Havnevik, Kjell J. (ed.) (1987). *The IMF and the World Bank in Africa.* Uppsala: Scandinavian Institute of African Studies.

Heinecke, P. (1986). *Popular Fallacies in the Nigerian Social Sciences.* Bendel State: S. Asekome Publishers.

Lesthaeghe, R. J. (ed.) (1989). *Reproduction and Social Organization in Sub-Saharan Africa.* Berkeley: University of California Press.

Lesthaeghe, R. J., Kaufmann, G. and Meekers, D. (1989). 'The nuptiality regimes in sub-Saharan Africa'. In Lesthaeghe (1989).

Lee, R. D. and Miller, T. (1990). 'Population growth, externalities to childbearing, and fertility policy in developing countries'. In *Proceedings of the World Bank Annual Conference on Development Economics*. Washington, DC: World Bank.

Mbachu, D. (1987). 'Nigeria: too many children?' *Africa/Asia*, 40 (April 1987).

McLean, S. and Efua, G. S. (eds) (1985). *Female Circumcision, Excision and Infibulation: the Facts and Proposals for Change*. The Minority Rights Group. Report No. 47. London : Pergamon Press (second revised edition; first edition 1980).

Nigerian Daily Times (1985). 7 November.

OECD (1987). *The Future of Migration*. Paris: OECD Publications.

Olinger, J. P. (1978). 'The World Bank and Nigeria,' *Review of African Political Economy*, 13 (May–August 1978).

Otobo, D. (1981). 'The Nigerian general strike'. *Review of African Political Economy*, 22 (October–December 1981).

Salas, R. M. (1985). *Reflections on Population*. New York: Pergamon Press (second edition).

Saro-Wiwa, Ken (1992). *Genocide in Nigeria*. Lagos: Saros International Publishers.

Serafini, A. (ed.) (1974). *L'operaio multinazionale in Europa*. Milan: Feltrinelli Editore.

Simmons, O. G. (1988). *Perspectives on Development and Population Growth in the Third World*. New York: Plenum Press.

Solanke, A. (1988). 'Illegal and dangerous'. *West Africa*, 31 October– 6 November.

United Nations Department of Internal Economic and Social Affairs. (1988). *Case Studies in Population Policy: Nigeria*. Population Policy Paper N.16. New York: United Nations.

United Nations Economic Commission for Africa (1984). Report of the Second African Population Conference.

US Department of Commerce (1989). *Foreign Economic Trends (FET)*. June.

West Africa (1988). 8 January.

Women in Nigeria (ed.) (1985a). *The WIN Document: Conditions of Women in Nigeria and Policy Recommendations to 2000 AD*. Zaria (Nigeria): Women in Nigeria.

Women in Nigeria (ed.) (1985b). *Women in Nigeria Today*. London: Zed Books.

World Bank (1984). *World Development Report 1984*. New York: Oxford University Press.

World Bank (1988). *World Development Report 1988*. Oxford: Oxford University Press.

World Bank (1989). *Sub-Saharan Africa: from Crisis to Stustainable Development*. Washington, DC: World Bank.

4

AFRICAN WOMEN, DEVELOPMENT AND THE NORTH–SOUTH RELATIONSHIP

Andrée Michel

The demystification of social prejudices accepted as objective facts is one of sociology's most interesting and promising functions: the sociology of the family, for example, received a strong impetus when its practitioners in the United States began unmasking prejudices taken as certainties. In the same way, the sociology of development pursued its demystifying task by researching the participation of women in Third World development, a sphere previously distorted by the myths propagated by some economic theories in which women's labour and its contribution to national income became invisible (Michel 1985). Women sociologists have shown that the production of subsistence by rural Third World women, far from being extraneous to the capitalistic production of commodities, is essential to it.

Thanks to the invisible work of wives, children, mothers and sisters, the farmers of the Third World can sell their products at prices that are 20–30 per cent lower, reflecting the lower cost of reproducing their labour power (Michel 1983).

More recently, some women sociologists, especially those working in Third World universities, have shown that the structure of international relations between industrial and non-industrial countries is influenced notably by sexual discrimination.

In this chapter I will try to evaluate this influence, starting from research I carried out among African women. First, I will examine how the Lomé Conventions regulating relations between the European Community and its ACP partners in Africa, the Pacific and the Caribbean have influenced these women. Second, I will examine the consequences of these conventions in the aftermath of International Monetary Fund (IMF) and World Bank intervention in the African countries.

From Independence to the First Lomé Convention

The first Lomé Convention between the European Community (EC) and the ACP countries was concluded in 1975. As far as Africa is concerned, it was concluded within the framework of a colonial past in which Africa had specialized in the export of unprocessed mineral and agricultural products. In those years, in fact, the African countries, even if independent, were still dominated by foreign interests linked to the old power line-up: 'the foreign enterprises (industries, banks, commercial enterprises) split up the African continent according to the colonial inheritance' (Michel, Fatoumata-Diarra and Agbessi-Dos Santos 1981).

Africa's 'extrovert' development, based on exports profitable to the traditional colonial power centres, was not intended to satisfy the primary needs of African people. Yet the Lomé Conventions were presented as advantageous to the African countries thanks to financial mechanisms such as the Stabex and the Sysmin which were said to assure the African countries minimum income levels through guaranteed EC prices for agricultural products and mineral products respectively. But the conventions were negotiated without allowing for any democratic control over how the funds created by the two mechanisms were to be used.

With the oil crisis, the price of oil increased considerably, and the oil producers entrusted their revenues to the European, American and Japanese banks. This was why Japan could offer ample credit facilities to the African states to 'develop' their nations. The choice of giant projects enabled foreign companies to obtain profits and the banks to put Africa into debt. But nothing was done for the primary needs of the women (education, health, family planning, equipment to help with domestic tasks, drinking-water supplies, etc.) because they weren't present at the North–South negotiations. Rural women who produce for family consumption, like craftworking women who produce objects for daily life, are forgotten because their labour is made invisible and given no consideration as a requisite for development.

The European Parliament (EP) criticized the results of the two Lomé Conventions on various grounds. According to the EP (1983), the following facts could be taken as established:

- Even though the ACP countries enjoyed privileged access to the European market, their share of the total volume of EC imports between 1976 and 1982 diminished;

- Industrial cooperation between the EC and ACP countries suffered serious deterioration; in 1982, industrial exports represented only 1–2 per cent of total ACP exports to Europe;

- Quantities of the major African food products fell, meaning that food production had failed to follow demographic growth;

- The Stabex had failed to compensate the ACP countries for the loss resulting from the low prices paid for export crops and, in any case, the contemplated credits were not enough to satisfy the demand for them from the ACP nations.

As African sociologists have shown, the situation proved unequivocally detrimental to their countries, and in particular to rural women. They were hit the hardest in that:

- The employment of African women is concentrated in the agricultural and tertiary sectors, while it is very low in the industrial sector;

- The increase in export crops has reduced the land area available for cultivation for domestic consumption and has denied women land, or given them land that is too far away for them to farm.

- In this way, the workload of women has grown heavier every day. Unicef (1985) has calculated that African rural women represent 80 per cent of all African working women and that they work 16–18 hours a day at harvest time (coffee, cocoa, etc.). In fact, apart from cultivating the products needed for self-consumption, they also work in their husbands' fields for crops destined for sale and use up at least 6–8 hours a day in fetching water, fetching wood for cooking, carrying out the various domestic chores, and looking after the children. Apart from all that, they must also set aside time to sell some food or handmade products in the village market.

- The low price of crops destined for sale has forced their husbands to emigrate to the city in search of work and a wage. Many women have thus had to take on the tasks of the head of family, further increasing their workload. Unicef reports that 'in the high-emigration regions, Senegal, Burkina-Faso and Zambia, since the husbands are away for most of the year (50 per cent in Zambia, 60 per cent in Lesotho)' (Unicef 1985: 92), the women are left with full responsibility for agricultural production.

- Women have been hit particularly hard by the criteria used for assigning public expenditure. For example, in 1981, 11 per cent of total public expenditure in the African states went on the military sector, when only 5 per cent went on health and 16 per cent on education (Unicef 1985: 92). In the 1970s, in fact, arms trading grew considerably, and Europe sold at least 20 per cent of the arms purchased by the Third World countries (Grip 1989).

Thus, despite some slow improvement in education for girls, in 1980, according to UNESCO, 70 per cent of African women were illiterate (cf. 50 per cent of men). The proportion of African girls attending primary school rose from 35 per cent in 1960 to 43 per cent in 1980, but Unicef adds that

in the African countries with low schooling, the girls are in a much more backward situation, and represent only a third or a quarter of the pupils. Drop-out rates are much higher for girls than for boys, and the difference between the number of girls and boys who sign up seems to be on the increase (Unicef 1985: 48).

As regards health, Unicef says that

after an initial improvement during the 1960s and the early 1970s, the indices began to fall.... Even though, in 1975–80, there was a slightly higher fall in the infant mortality rate in the sub-Saharan countries compared to the other LDC countries, their infantile mortality rate was still 127 per cent of the average rate for the LDC countries as a whole (Unicef 1985: 10).

Women's health, in particular the health of pregnant and breast-feeding women, was precarious because of nutritional insufficiency, and maternal mortality was high because of lack of assistance in labour. Life expectancy in Africa was only 48 years (Unicef 1985: 81).

Moreover, international statistics ignore the price paid by women in the international, civil and tribal wars that have broken out in this period in all the sub-Saharan African countries. After the world wars, Europe has preferred to export war rather than suffer it directly; the African states buy arms and make liberal use of them. African women pay a very high direct and indirect price: from the hunger caused by evacuation since they can no longer cultivate land for the family to the famine provoked by the invasions of locusts which reproduce in areas of guerilla warfare (Ethiopia, Sudan, Mauritania) where chemical pest control is no longer possible; and to violence of various types, from genocide to collective rape. A sociologist from Chad has shown that the civil war in that country has also brought a growth in prostitution among very young girls and an increase in clitoridectomy. The silence blanketing these crimes perpetrated against women can no longer continue to hide the extent to which they are the fruit of a perverse 'development' based on a growth of commerce in which there is no distinction with respect to the type of commodity – for example, arms – traded.

Under the Guidance of the World Bank and the International Monetary Fund

From the start of the 1980s, it became clear that there would be no real inversion of the trend in Euro-African relations because the successive Lomé Conventions regulating economic exchanges between Europe and Africa were controlled and dominated by the power of the IMF and the World Bank. At the end of 1983, 25 African countries which had contracted heavy debts in the previous period accepted a structural adjustment programme drawn up by the World Bank and a stabilization programme with the IMF:

> the common aim of these programmes is to stabilize the balance-of-payments, extinguish the debt and reduce inflation. National objectives such as the creation and protection of jobs, guarantees for a minimum family income, and the provision of basic public services become secondary (Unicef 1985: 21).

This new stage of development, as we now know, was functional to the transfer of African resources to the industrial countries as debt payments. It is clear how far the Fourth Lomé Convention (December 1989) subordinated the financial aid promised to the sub-Saharan countries by the EC to the same colonialist conditions as those imposed by the IMF and the World Bank for their 'assistance' to the indebted African countries. Tubiana (1989) observes:

> The new programme of assistance for 'adjustment' will be more ample than in the past, and less rigidly tied to drastic conditions, even if these will in fact be very close to the criteria of assignation established by the IMF and the World Bank.

This meant that, over and above European speeches about the need to help Africa, the international banks' new and inhuman economic criteria would regulate Euro-African economic and political relations from that moment on.

The conditions required by these banks for granting credits or giving economic aid to the African countries were as follows (George 1988):

- An increase in national revenue from higher exports of agricultural and mineral products, and hence the assignation of more land to export crops (coffee, cocoa, cotton, etc.), removing it from cultivation for domestic consumption;

- Lower public expenditure on social needs (education, health, transport, etc.), but not necessarily accompanied by a decrease in the funds spent on imports of luxury goods and arms; cuts in state subsidies designed to keep down the price of the basic foodstuffs (oil, flour, rice, etc.) consumed by the poor; a wage freeze for workers and state white-collar workers with the simultaneous deregulation of prices; and the restructuring of public enterprises with the firing of thousands of employees;

- The opening of national frontiers to foreign imports in order to promote international trade, the generalized elimination of customs tariffs on imports, and currency devaluation.

All these are policies demanded by the international banks in support of the programme. And it is self-evident how they rest on sexually discriminatory criteria which reflect the North's power logic. In fact, it is common knowledge to what extent the poor African countries' debt has weighed them down with financial commitments towards the wealthy countries, just as it is common knowledge how far officials in each indebted African country have run the structural adjustment and stabilization programmes so that the debt's cost would not fall on the élite, but on the poor, and especially the poor women.

Unicef, the World Bank and the European Parliament have themselves recognized that these programmes had deleterious effects on the African people. As early as 1985, Unicef reported that the results had been the opposite of what was intended:

> These programmes have deepened the economic crisis and generated human crises; unemployment has increased, the income of the poorer social strata has fallen, import-linked industries have reduced their production, public services have been reduced, and public discontent and political instability have increased (Unicef 1985: 21).

It could not have been otherwise, since those same programmes, imposed by the IMF and the World Bank on most of the indebted developing countries, lowered the prices of the agricultural products they exported to the North, placed supplementary export revenue at the disposition of the speculators and *rentier* social groups, and increased interest rates, annulling the earlier sacrifices made by the African states so they could pay their debts.

In 1989 the World Bank, the fundamental actor in this drama, reported that the food gap in Africa was widening and then involved about 100 million of a total of 450 million inhabitants. At the same time, unemployment was increasing in step with the growth of the cities (about 30 will have more than a million inhabitants by the end of the century), and the population explosion was emerging as a 'delayed action bomb' in an environment that was already extensively damaged (Fottorino 1989). The Bank's experts in fact forecast that, in 1995, African revenues would be lower than in the 1970s (De Barrin 1989).

The European Parliament's conclusion as regards the 1980s was as discouraging as the World Bank's: 'For the African countries, this decade has been a decade of "regression" and "lost hopes"' (Wurtz 1989). In fact, there was a drop in African living standards of 25 per cent compared to 1980, with 85 per cent of the population living under the poverty line (Wurtz 1989). The same European Parliament report indicated that, during the 1980s, there was a fall in agricultural production and an important increase in food imports, which means greater dependence, coupled with an almost total absence of industrial production (apart, perhaps, from small industry for consumption) and an overall decline in services, especially those concerned with human reproduction, starting with health and education. With the fall in the price of basic products, there was also a deterioration in the terms of trade, while the African countries lost a third of their European markets (Wurtz 1989). To this situation was added a fall in public aid from the EC countries (Wurtz 1989). Moreover, between 1980 and 1988, military expenditure in the African countries may have dropped by 50 per cent, but it still represented the most important item in the national budget, to the extent that it compromised the growth of the gross national product (GNP):

> To stabilize the product *per capita* means increasing the portion of GNP devoted to investment by 3 points. These missing 3 points represent the part destined by sub-Saharan Africa to military expenditure (Grellet 1988).

But these same structural adjustment and stabilization programmes have created a situation so explosive that the Third World states feel obliged to invest in arms in order to keep it at tolerable levels:

> It's a vicious circle: repression brings recession which makes the social difficulties bitterer, which in turn leads to an increase in the system of repression (Grellet 1988).

The World Bank's president, who has recognized that the Third World's military expenditures represent a third of the debt service paid by these same states each year, has asked them to reduce military spending by $200 million a year so the money can be spent on eradicating poverty (*Jornal do Brasil* 27 September 1989).

The Consequences of Structural Adjustment for African Women

A feminist approach to study and intervention in this field must start by bringing into focus the consequences of the IMF's structural adjustment and stabilization programmes for African women. In fact, as Peggy Antrobus wrote recently, the new policies of the IMF, the World Bank and the Lomé Conventions continue to be defined on the basis of traditional sexual prejudices:

- It is as if they were ignorant of the essential interrelationship between the women's productive and reproductive functions, and the extent to which production is linked, not only to capital, technology and markets, but also to the fundamental physical, psychological and intellectual capacities of human beings (Antrobus 1989) – capacities that are developed in children by women, first as mothers and family educators, then as teachers and educators.

- It is as if they were not aware of the important and direct contributions that women make through their central position in production, as producers of the fundamental domestic consumer goods and as workers in the formal and informal sectors of industry, commerce and the services (Antrobus 1989).

By continuing to ignore the labour content of women's role and by continuing to slash services (kindergartens, maternal schools, child-care centres, health centres, family planning centres, public services for the handicapped and the infirm, etc.) from the public budget, the new policies reassign the responsibility and onus of these services to the women, whose workload is thus made that much heavier. In these programmes, everything is planned as if structural adjustment was targeted against women's rights and women's welfare.

Apart from increasing the workload, adjustment has imposed other notable privations and further suffering on women:

- Since the beginning of structural adjustment in the 1980s, in various African countries, child malnutrition has increased and child mortality has stopped falling (Unicef 1985: 27). In the sub-Saharan countries, maternal mortality in 1989 was the highest in the world. Fran Hosken explains this precisely in terms of the reduction in health services, particularly in maternity wards in hospitals. In 1989, Fran Hosken visited them and compared the situation to the one she found on her previous visit:

following the measures imposed by the IMF and the World Bank, there was a drastic reduction in the budget of hospitals funded by the African governments and in all health services. The maternity wards in Africa were already neglected and suffered from every imaginable shortcoming, but they were now close to losing all their functions: they had no medicines, no health equipment, nor even any qualified staff, who had gone elsewhere because they had been left without wages (Hosken 1989).

- The fertility index of African women is the highest in the world, with an average conception rate of 6.6, yet family planning services reach only 10 per cent of the women in the fertile age group, and one of the consequences of this grave shortcoming in services is the 'maternal exhaustion syndrome', which has been recognized by international institutions (Unicef 1985: 43).

- The growth of AIDS in African women has been dramatic. The international conference on AIDS held in Paris in 1989 confirmed:

  there is an enormous discrepancy between official speeches on the importance of guaranteeing the health of mothers and children, and the means in fact adopted for achieving the aim. Health in the world, and above all health policy, is made by men for men (*Le Monde* 29 November 1989).

- Between 1980 and 1985, even though the literacy rate among women improved, they were still strongly discriminated against by comparison with men. The rate for women fell by 4 points, from 70 per cent to 66 per cent, while for men it dropped 3 points, from 50 per cent to 47 per cent (Leger Sivard 1985). In November 1989, a preliminary report from the ILO (International Labour Organization) summed up the 'de-schooling' of Africa and warned that the budget shares devoted to education in the African countries are the lowest in the world. As regards primary education, the growth rate of education had been reduced both because of population growth and because of the effects of the World Bank/IMF policies, which aggravated the problem notably.

In most of Africa's rural areas, one might find what happened in Tanzania, where people began to 'educate only the male children, thus renewing the colonialist tradition of giving the girls fewer educational opportunities' (Meena 1988). This discrimination between children widened in step with the application of the restrictive policies, and in many African countries the upshot was the introduction of paid education, which fully justifies pessimistic forecasts as to the improvement of education for females.

- Unemployment has hit both sexes, but the men more extensively since there are more of them in the labour market. For this reason, an increasing number of wives and mothers are obliged to look for paid work, in the formal or informal sectors. Even if at the cost of a heavier workload, this new role has introduced a trend towards the redefinition of sexual roles within the couple. As Zene Tadesse writes (1988):

> The crisis opens up new opportunities and, although little documentation is available, even the more patriarchal of men are beginning to understand that, if it weren't for the women's ingenuity, the family would not exist. There is a strong tendency to revolutionize the family income model, which in the past was under the privileged terrain of the head of the family.

Moreover, the working role of African women does not end with what they do for the family's survival: recent research shows the extent to which, in the African continent, they contribute to collective labour in the general interest of the the local community. In other words, they contribute to creating a new type of development, managed and directed in the first person, a development that is no longer 'extrovert', but is envisaged by and for the African people. The Unicef report indicates that

> in many countries – Ethiopia, Kenya, Lesotho, Mali, Nigeria, Tanzania – the women contribute to the creation of water plants, participate in construction projects, in Burkina-Faso, for example (earth barrages), and Malawi (water piping), etc. Moreover, in Angola, Malawi, and Lesotho, control and maintenance of manual pumps are entrusted to the women. There must be exploration of other opportunities throughout the African continent in which everyone, but the women in particular, can participate (Unicef 1985: 48).

Zene Tadesse, again, stresses how African women's decisive role in the survival of the family group gives them sentiments of pride and dignity:

> the women begin to see that their contribution is indispensable. In the past, precisely because of an ideology that underestimated their contribution, the women tended to interiorize this concept. All that is changing. It's not precisely a victory since it means excess work and excess fatigue, but it gives women a sense of their value (Tadesse 1988).

Strategies for a Feminist Intervention

In the states that became independent in the 1960s, the new form of control over Africa by the international banks has replaced domination by the old colonial powers, but it has created no counter-trend against the lack of African development. Rather, in Africa, it has 'developed' more hunger, more poverty, and more debt-linked dependence on the industrial countries. Even if the structural adjustment imposed by the banks has forced African women to exercise new family and economic roles and, with them, has developed their self-esteem, this cannot be seen as a satisfying target achieved from the women's viewpoint, since they want, not only to survive, but also to live and to stop paying such a high price for survival. How can this objective be achieved?

Diana Elson (1987) suggests that the African Women's Bureaux created by various African governments should enjoy full participation in the debates and decisions at summit meetings between government institutions and international organizations and banks. This is an idea urged by some of the industrial countries' institutional representatives, including one from the European Parliament, a member of the development committee, who said explicitly that future programmes 'must be established more evidently on principles of participation, which means reaching agreement rather than simply communicating decisions after the fact' (Wurtz 1989). Evidently, feminists from the industrial and non-industrial countries will need to struggle if they want equality of women's participation with the men's.

This is the strategy that should be adopted, not only whenever the EC members meet African leaders, but also when these meet IMF and World Bank negotiators. But is it right to reduce women's participation to that of the African Women's Bureaux alone? We would think not, because it would be ineffective. In fact, these women are part of the African countries' state structures and, as such, must first of all defend the state's interests rather than the welfare and primary needs of African women. They can defend the interests of women only within the strict limits defined by 'reasons of state', which in the last analysis are the reasons of the privileged who hold economic, political and military power.

In my opinion, it would be good if the women of the Women's Bureaux could join with the women of the pressure groups in the developing and industrial countries that are completely independent of 'reasons of state'. These pressure groups may be non-governmental organizations (NGOs) or other organizations, since not even being an NGO is a guarantee of independence from 'reasons of state'. According to Peggy Antrobus, and I agree, while European policies continue to compromise North–South relations gravely, many women do not share their 'colonialist' approach. Women of the North share with women of the South the feeling that this reality is something alien to them. To be the segregated and subordinated 'second sex' is both their common condition and an excellent basis for collective work.

This should consist in exchanges of information, the creation of pressure groups capable of influencing governments, and the organization of exchanges between women.[1] For example, DAWN in the South and WIDE in the North could become women's pressure groups and establish a common position for when debt problems and Euro-African relations are discussed. These groups could claim participation with full rights when the African and European leaders meet for negotiations on economic problems. Other women's pressure groups with full participation rights could include women's cooperatives and mutual aid collectives.

In my view, three conditions have to be satisfied if these pressure groups are in fact to promote women's welfare effectively:

1 Their members should be very well informed on each country's economic, political and social situation and on the needs of the poorer African women, their collective survival organizations, and their capabilities and aspirations for training in agriculture, craftwork, industry and the services. This means that the pressure groups must be integrated, with participation not only from qualified researchers (women economists, nutrition experts, sociologists, doctors, etc.), but also from peasant women and poor and illiterate women from the cities who know what women's non-negotiable needs truly are – what Third World researchers call the 'bottom up approach'.

2 A feminist perspective should be introduced into the 'bottom up approach' since it is not enough for the women in the pressure groups to consider development models different from those traditionally imposed by Europe on Africa. In learning their trade from universities in the developing as well as the industrial countries, African economists of both sexes have in fact learned to share the sexist premises of precisely those models for the economy and development that have also failed to give economic independence or satisfy primary needs. This is one good reason why feminists should be admitted as social actors in Euro-African negotiations, because by coming to identify economic theory's concealment of their social and economic value in non-market production, they have come to reject that theory's sexist principles.

It is certainly not our aim to limit the roles of African women to the traditional family ones, but one should consider that, for them, 'development' means, above all, easier access to health and family planning centres, drinking water and water plant, and the promise of equipment that can lighten their workload. Instead of the massive projects that make profits for small African élites, 'development' should be, above all, the means for satisfying the primary needs of unprivileged people, particularly the women since it is they who are most active in ensuring family survival. African women should have the same civil and political rights as men and should enjoy recognition of the same property rights, above all as far as concerns the land.

For feminists, 'development' also means that African women and men should have equal education and training from the schools and professional centres, so that they can share jobs and domestic tasks equally. So, we repeat, the presence of European or African women in the negotiations will not improve the situation of African women if the feminist perspective is not accepted in the 'bottom up approach'. But this perspective does not imply that all African couples should be obliged to share domestic, social and professional tasks, only that they should have a greater opportunity to share domestic, social and professional roles more fairly and with greater justice.

3 The feminist 'bottom up approach' should find its focal point in the principle that the distribution of resources is as important as their production. It should point to the fair assignation of resources between Africa and Europe, between the social classes, and between the sexes in every country.

The problem of the allocation of resources concerns both the debt and the sharing of public expenditure in each African country (debt exacts a higher cost from the poorer countries and, within these, the poorer social strata, and the women pay more than the men because the reduction in public services hits them first of all). European feminists and African women cannot tolerate that a preponderant share of public expenditure in Africa should go on military expenditure to the detriment of health and education. It is unacceptable that the price of the African export crops should be so low (in 1989, the price of coffee diminished by 50 per cent and of cocoa by 40 per cent), forcing the peasants to leave their fields and emigrate to the big cities while the rural women are left as their family's sole support, increasing their workload even further. It is intolerable that the prices of manufactured products exported to Africa by the EC should be increasing at the same time.

The sharing of resources between poor and wealthy countries, between social classes, and between the sexes should be the feminist perspective central to the 'bottom up approach', a perspective that is necessary for building just and peaceful societies in both Africa and Europe.

Notes

1 Speech delivered by Peggy Antrobus during a press conference organized by the WHO on 4 December 1989 at Copenhagen with the participation of DAWN (Development Alternatives With Women) and WIDE (Women In Development/Europe).

Bibliography

Antrobus, P. (1989). 'Wanted: women in Lomé'. In Lomé briefing, 10 September.

De Barrin, J. (1989). 'Afrique', *Le Monde*, 28 November 1989.

Elson, D. (1987). *The Impact of Structural Adjustment on Women: Concepts and Issues*. London: Institute for African Alternatives.

European Paliament (1983). *Le Parlement européen et le Tiers Monde*. Brussels: Bureau d'information du Parlement européen, Division des Publications.

Fottorino, E. (1989). 'Un rapport de la Banque Mondiale'. *Le Monde*, 28 November 1989.

George, S. (1988). 'Jusqu'au cou. Enquête sur la dette du Tiers-Monde'. Paris: La Découverte.

Grellet, G. (1988). 'Les épées plus que les épis'. *Le Monde*, 12 January 1988.

Grip. (1989). *L 'Europe des Armes*. Bruxelles.

Hosken, F. P. (1989). 'Safe motherhood'. Conference paper at Niamey (Niger). In *Women International Network* (*WIN News*), 15, 2.

Jornal do Brasil (1989). 'Bird Pede ao 3° Mundo Final de Gasto com Armes'. 27 September.

Le Monde. 'Le Sida et la mère'. 29 September 1989.

Leger Sivard, R. (1985). *Women. A World Survey*. New York: Carnegie, Ford and Rockefeller Foundations.

Meena, R. (1988). 'Women and debt: the Tanzanian experience'. Utrecht: Veso, Noord Zuid Campagne.

Michel, A. (1983). 'Multinationales et inégalité de classe et de sexe'. *Current Sociology*, special number, 31, 1 (Spring).

Michel, A. (1985). 'Dix ans d'irruption des sciences humaines dans le domaine du travail des paysannes'. *Tiers-Monde*, 36, 102 (April–June).

Michel, A., Fatoumata-Diarra, A. and Agbessi-Dos Santos, H. (1981). *Femmes et Multinationales*. Paris: Karthala.

PE (Parlement européen). (1983). *Le Parlement européen et le Tiers Monde*,

Bureau d'information du Parlement européen, Division des Publications, Bruxelles.

Tadesse, Z. (1988). 'Structural adjustment policies and their impact on women' In WIDE, *Why Women Worldwide Pay the Price*. Oxford.

Tubiana, L. (1989). 'Le changement dans la continuité'. In *Solagral*, 87 (December).

Unicef (1985). *Un avenir pour les enfants d'Afrique*. New York.

Wurtz, F. (1989). 'Les Acp pris entre le marteau protectionniste et l'enclume de l'ultra-libéralisme'. *Le Courrier*, CE, Bruxelles, 18 (November–December).

5

PAUPERIZATION AND WOMEN'S PARTICIPATION IN SOCIAL MOVEMENTS IN BRAZIL

Alda Britto da Motta
Inaiá Maria Moreira de Carvalho

In recent years, students of socio-economic trends have successfully traced the course of the selective impoverishment of sectors of the Brazilian people. With few exceptions, however, the significance of this impoverishment from the point of view of the specific groups affected has not received adequate treatment. This chapter points to this deficiency in one area, that of women's increasing pauperization and their political answer to it.

The first part of the chapter elaborates in detail the causes, currents, and course of Brazilian pauperization; in the second part we consider what these changes have meant for women, and how women have responded to the trend.

One of the majors aspects of Brazil in recent decades has been its socially exclusionary character. Although authoritarianism and marked social inequalities have been constant features of the country's entire history, since the 1960s they have become even more evident and severe, if we consider such events as the collapse of populism, the establishment of a repressive military regime that lasted for over twenty years (from 1964 to 1986), the downfall of this regime and the troubled transition into a formal democracy.

The underlying authoritarian character and overall goals of the military regime were clearly spelled out in the structuring of a bureaucratic-authoritarian state and in the policies then implemented. The state imposed a 'new' model of development in which the process of economic expansion and modernization led to changes whose scope, magnitude, and repercussions should not be underestimated.

Under military rule, monopoly capital expanded and advanced

significantly, spurring the growth, diversification and thorough transformation of the Brazilian structure of production, which came to lean heavily on large industry and related modern services. Growth and modernization also spread into the countryside, through the creation of large agro-industrial firms. As a result, the Brazilian economy experienced a dramatic boom; in the 1970s, in fact, talk was of a Brazilian 'economic miracle', and even today, in spite of the current economic crisis, Brazil is still ranked as the world's eighth largest economy.

In the course of these changes, Brazil also became a predominantly urban country. The labour market expanded and diversified; and the occupational and class structures evidenced substantial redefinition, marked by the emergence of new social actors and their corresponding values, attitudes, interests and conflicts.

The vicious character of the economic development of Brazil and its social consequences have been widely recognized. As is well known, one of the main pillars of the 'miracle' was the severe wage squeeze policy implemented by the government, made possible by the existing abundance of labour as well as by the state's overtly authoritarian character. The military rulers openly sought the demobilization of society, not only through censorship of the media, but also through direct attempts to destroy, control and/or repress labour union activities and expressions of popular will, thus ensuring the passivity and silence of the majority.

These actions, combined with the conservative modernization of the countryside and the sealing off of agricultural frontiers (brought about by speculation built on the commercial enterprises of large landowners) led to considerable growth in the country's national wealth. But this accomplishment came only at the expense of the labouring classes; there was a drastic decline in the real value of wages, as well as a significant rise in the rates of underemployment and unemployment.

Already evident in the 1970 census data, which clearly depicted the marked increase in income concentration, these phenomena generated heated debates. Thus, even at the peak of the 'miracle', General Garrastazu Medici, then President of Brazil, was forced to admit that: 'The economy is doing fine, but not the people.'

Nonetheless, this official recognition of the increasing pauperization of the Brazilian working classes and of the masses at large did not translate into effective governmental action geared towards reversing the situation, or even attenuating some of its more drastic effects. On the contrary, top priority continued to be assigned to programmes and investments directed to the needs of capitalist expansion, while criteria guiding supposedly 'social' policies were still efficiency, viability and rationalization. In certain cases, in fact, these policies openly served the interests of particular business sectors. A blatant example was the housing policy: it accrued many more benefits to the financial sector, the civil construction industry, and to middle- and higher-income home buyers than to the genuinely needy. Likewise, the national health policy not only shuffled preventive medical care and basic sanitation into the background, but actually promoted the privatization of medical services. Meanwhile, the lack of financial resources, increasing bureaucratization and chronic inefficiency of public services, along with clientelistic practices in the implementation of state programmes, combined to disable efforts for compensatory measures (Carvalho and Laniado 1989).

It is important to note, however, that even in the 1970s this pattern of development was already showing signs of wearing out. In the 1980s – which have been depicted by Brazilian economists as the 'lost decade' – the crisis became more evident and severe, aggravated as it was by the effects of the international oil crisis, mounting foreign and national debts, and by ever-increasing inflation rates.

While the economic crisis eroded the foundation of the military regime, other social and political factors – most notably the rise of wide-spread popular protest for redemocratization – speeded up its demise and downfall. The so-called 'democratic transition' phase followed with the establishment of the 'New Republic', and the elaboration of a new constitution. Along with these changes, some hopes emerged for a new direction in economic planning where social priorities would be considered and the ongoing trend towards social exclusion and polarization reversed.

Unfortunately, these expectations were soon frustrated by the restrictions imposed by the crisis, as well as by the character of the transition itself. As several studies have pointed out (O'Donnell 1982; Moura 1989; Carvalho and Laniado 1989; Carmargo and Diniz 1989), the strategy of gradual, peaceable transition has not allowed for more profound and significant ruptures in the existing power bloc, or in the patterns of development adopted by the military regime. Based on a gentlemen's agreement which effectively limited itself to the removal of the military from centre stage and the re-enactment of formal democratic processes, the new regime could neither foster substantive changes in relations between the state and the impoverished masses nor grant to the emerging democracy the social dimension inherent in modern liberal states.

Thus, at present, Brazil faces an unprecedented crisis in a context of adverse reorganization of international economic power blocs, a situation in which Latin America has not succeeded in gaining ground. Moreover, the internal crisis goes beyond the economic sphere: it is also a political and moral crisis, as reflected by current power disputes and the clear absence of a larger social project that could rally different social factions around a new pattern of development.

In the midst of this crisis, President Fernando Collor has assumed a neo-liberal position, assigning top priority to fighting inflation by means of orthodox measures such as budget cuts and other strongly recessive measures which have already resulted in enormous social costs.[1]

Pauperization and Subsistence Conditions

The evolution and different dimensions of poverty in Brazil have been analysed in several works, as data referring to the more recent years are obtainable from official statistical records. Thus, according to a study conducted by Matarazzo Suplicy between 1961 and 1973, while the country's *per capita* income rose by 58 per cent, the real minimum wage decreased in value by more than 55 per cent. In the years that followed, the situation continued to worsen: data included in the 1981 National Domestic Unit Survey (PNAD) showed that 50 per cent of the poorest Brazilians classified as economically active earned only 13.4 per cent of the total national income, which meant that, in that year (1981), their *per capita* income did not surpass US$1,200. In 1989, a similar survey revealed that these values had decreased to 10.4 per cent and US$900 respectively, whereas the income held by the most wealthy 5 per cent jumped from a total of 33.4 per cent in 1981, to 39.4 per cent in 1989 (IBGE, 1981 and 1989 PNADs).

Given this sharp intensification of income concentration, it is not surprising that, in 1986, 40 per cent of the total Brazilian population were classed below the poverty level, while 18 per cent were found to live below minimum poverty standards, as depicted in a study conducted by the United Nations Economic Commission for Latin America and the Caribbean (CEPAL 1986).

As some of our own studies have shown (Carvalho 1984; 1987), increasing pauperization has had a significant impact upon the everyday lives of the labouring classes, in that it has:

• Forced a reduction in subsistence costs and in the cost of the reproduction of labour, as well as a severe contraction in consumption patterns, leading to the degradation of the quality of life of working-class families, to the point of depriving them of basic necessities such as food and clean water;

• Caused a corresponding increase in the number of working hours needed to meet the rising cost of the subsistence needs of workers and their families. This has demanded that the working day of those who act as household heads (mainly men, but increasingly women as well) be extended, either through putting in extra working hours in their regular jobs, or by doing odd jobs on the side. Yet, since there are obvious limits to the working day – including biological limits, of course – increasing pauperization has progressively demanded the incorporation of other members of the household into the labour force as the only other means of offsetting the diminishing value of the principal provider's wages.

In addition, such processes cannot be dissociated from the continued absence of public policies and lack of public commitment to providing for collective consumption services such as education, health, basic sanitation, transportation and public housing, which could absorb part of the costs of the reproduction of labour. This has created an even greater burden on the already traumatized budgets of the working classes.

POVERTY AND THE SEXUAL DIVISION OF LABOUR

In turning to the question of how pauperization of the Brazilian people has specifically affected conditions for women, we argue that the changes under discussion have contributed to renewed difficulties for women's struggles, particularly with respect to their participation in the labour force and involvement in urban social movements.

As has been widely noted, the traditional patterns of the sexual division of labour also have spatial dimensions: whereas men have been 'freed' to join the labour market and be incorporated into production as well as to undertake activities, political and otherwise, generally associated with the 'public' sphere, women have been confined to the domestic world – to the 'private' sphere – and entrusted with those tasks and activities most linked to the so-called process of reproduction, namely, with the unpaid production of use values needed for the daily subsistence and reproduction of the family which, precisely because they are 'unpaid' and performed within the private sphere, are in general socially devalued. The division of labour by sex also explains, in great part, women's traditionally restricted social participation. Thus, in Brazil, until recently, women's participation in the labour force was not only relatively small, but generally limited to working-class women and to those occupations ideologically associated with their traditional roles in the family and in subsistence production.

The growing pressures of the process of pauperization and of the depicted crisis, however, have contributed to changes in the picture, if only in quantitative terms. In the last decades, in fact, the rate of women's participation in the labour force has shown visible growth. In 1970, for instance, women represented a mere 20.7 per cent of the total economically active population. In 1980, however, this percentage had risen to 27.7 per cent, climbing to 33.5 per cent in 1985, and to 34.7 per cent in 1987.[2]

The changes resulting from economic development have created new job opportunities for working-class women in areas such as maintenance and cleaning services linked to the formal sector as well as in certain industrial sectors, but still symbolically linked to those tasks commonly defined as 'feminine'. Likewise, those changes have not translated into the liberation of women from the domestic world, nor contributed to the development of a greater social consciousness among women. Moreover, the male labour force is still considerably larger, and, historically, men have always constituted the segment of 'preferred' workers. On the other hand, the incorporation of women into production frequently conflicts with their domestic responsibilities, complicating the feasibility of their participation in the labour force, at least on a regular, stable basis.

Despite the noted changes, therefore, women are still concentrated in few occupations, such as family-based agricultural production, paid domestic service, traditional industry, petty commerce, and/or in other unskilled and poorly paid occupations in the service sector. Many of these occupations, in fact, can be juggled together with the performance of domestic tasks since they can be carried out in an autonomous fashion, that is, at women's own homes, in their own time, and on a discontinuous basis, thus being flexible and easily adaptable to domestic duties. Other such occupations include laundry services at home, and petty commerce in alcoholic drinks and prepared foods in the housefront shops commonly found in most poor neighbourhoods throughout Brazil.

It is also important to note that these phenomena are not merely economic, but also have social and political implications. Though involved in income-generating activities, women still remain confined to the domestic sphere, either physically or ideologically, thus defining themselves primarily as housewives and mothers, while men are self-defined primarily as workers (Kergoat 1978; Safa 1989; Caldeira 1990). It is not surprising, therefore, that the 1988 PNAD revealed that men represented 66.2 per cent of all Brazilians affiliated with labour unions and/or associations, and women only 33.8 per cent. In the specific case of labour unions, the contrast was even greater, as far as the rates of membership were concerned: 78.1 per cent for men compared to 21.9 per cent for women (IBGE, 1988 PNAD).

In spite of women's seemingly low levels of membership in professional associations and political parties, and of their participation in the political arena in general, and despite the fact that some studies have depicted them as more conservative than men,[3] women play a significant role in a 'new' form of collective action and articulation; that is, in the so-called urban social movements.

The Emergence of Social Movements

Since the mid-1970s, a number of popular manifestations and/or movements organized in response to collective demands have emerged, especially in the larger cities, São Paulo in particular. They have usually been centred in residential areas, particularly working-class neighbourhoods, generally located in city outskirts (*periferia*). While some groups demonstrate the considerable influence of the Catholic Church,[4] they nonetheless bear the markings of secular social relations and everyday currents.

Though one cannot establish a direct cause-and-effect relationship, it cannot be denied that these movements are closely linked to increased impoverishment and the noted lack of collective consumer services, resulting from deficient governmental policy. The manifestations, in fact, have usually been directed at the state, and their demands include better education, health, sanitation and transportation services, as well as access to the use of city-owned properties (for home building) and public housing.[5]

The frequency, visibility and overall characteristics of such movements and popular manifestations were something of a novelty on the Brazilian political scene of the 1970s, drawing the attention of scholars and researchers, and generating hopes for change on the part of more progressive politicians.

In questioning the notion of a supposedly frail civil society before the (authoritarian) state, in producing 'new' political actors and a 'new' praxis, these movements were seen, at first, as if endowed with positive attributes for renewal – and thus with ample possibilities in terms of social advancement and change (Carvalho and Laniado, 1990). More recently, however, their shortcomings and limitations – and those of the earlier analyses – have become more evident. But it cannot be denied that they have played an important role in revitalizing the dynamics of Brazilian politics. In particular, they engendered a revalorization of the day-to-day living experiences of the working classes, revealing how pauperization, social exclusion and domination are reflected in people's needs and wants; and how the network of social relations is congregated and expressed in the practices, symbols and individual and collective experiences that are also relevant to the viability of social struggles – and not necessarily to those struggles found in great historical moments.

Beyond this, the revalorization of everyday life has broadened the political field, opening new perspectives on the constitution and expression of the notion of citizenship, laying the basis for a more democratic political culture. Furthermore, these movements made possible the articulation (as collective actors) of those social segments categorically marginalized from the political scene since time immemorial for lack of means of articulation. Such was the case of enormous contingents of working-class women.

Women and Social Movements

The new focus on everyday life which the analyses of social movements officially heralded complemented the theoretical path traced by feminist analysis – a fact which underlines the potential and necessity of the social production of knowledge at this historical moment.

As such, in the last decades, the unfolding of grassroots movements and the on-the-ground roles played by women in such movements have crosscut if not utterly collapsed into each other, and all the more so as women constitute ever larger percentages of the participants.

As noted earlier, the participation of women in formal organizations such as labour unions and political parties, though expanding, is still relatively low. However, their presence is significantly greater in less formal and less hierarchical organizations such as urban movements and neighbourhood associations. The key to this phenomenon no doubt lies exactly there – that is, precisely in the informal character of these organizations, and in the possibility for creating new social relations, similar to the primary relationships (Souza Lobo 1987; Durhan 1984).

It is evident that pauperization and the economic crisis lie at the roots of the processes under discussion. But since political activity has historically been alien to women, the rupturing of the ideological barriers could only be achieved at the collective level – as it actually has been – and through more familiar paths, closer to the daily personal experiences of women, such as through neighbour relations. At the same time, this articulation takes place, initially, on the basis of the traditional female roles (Alvarez 1990), which means that women organize themselves from the outset, even if not consciously, through gender as well through class principles.

Without a previous awareness that they are joining an organization, women instead view their activities in terms of working with their friends and neighbours towards the improvement of living conditions and neighbourhood services. It is mainly as mothers and housewives – the fundamental adult female identity – that women are mobilized. As in Caldeira's (1984) much-cited remark, in São Paulo,

> Women from the Jardim das Camèlias did not see the slightest problem in demanding childcare and health centres, nor in going to the meetings ... since they interpreted all of this as 'working for the welfare of my children'. Thus, it was as responsible mothers that they were able to take over the mayor's office, in the same manner that the fact of being conscious mothers allows them to leave home more easily to 'face the outside world' to work.

There are a number of similar testimonies, but the desire to get out of the house and away from the drudgery and routine of domestic chores, to go and have some fun and meet (other) people, are also widely manifested. The desire for greater sociability, therefore, is another important factor in mobilizing women, as expressed in testimonies from the poor neighbourhoods of Salvador (Bahia):

> I find it pleasant to do neighbourhood work. This work gets you out of women's perpetual prison: the home (CEAS 1981).

> Some women find it 'empty' just to take care of children and wash and iron – it is plain emptiness. Thus they feel they need to get out of that routine. They have no other place to go, and they want to grow. At least, they can find friends here (CEAS 1978).

> I like to go out to the streets, I like to go out to fight for things. I like to be among people, talking, making demands (Interview in Britto Da Motta 1990).

It is also important to remember that poor women have always maintained solidarity and mutual aid networks in their neighbourhoods (Britto Da Motta 1977). In Bahia, besides participating in church-related activities, women also have a long history of involvement in collective squatters' movements. These movements and the resulting squatters' settlements (or *invasões*), were actually the initial core for the emergence of most of the poor, working-class neighbourhoods in Salvador.

Entrusted with the responsibility of domestic consumption needs, women are not only in charge of balancing the family budget and attending to the necessary shopping, but also forced to enter into direct contact with government institutions. And not simply to make use of the public services cited earlier – education, health care, transportation – but, more recently, to get needed foodstuffs, not covered by the family budget, donated through specific state-run social programmes. Thus, according to Jelin (1990), 'the organization of living conditions is a real or potential area of female participation'.

By the same token, the chronic lack of services is perceived by women as being part of their immediate family concerns. Reflecting upon their roles as housewives and mothers, many women point out that:

> My husband sometimes tries to stop me from going to the meetings. But I always try to show to him that this is part of a woman's duty. After all, we are the ones who see the major problems in the neighbourhood. Not all men are aware that there are not sufficient schools, nor decent water, or that there are kids playing in the middle of the garbage. So, it is up to women to fight for improvements in the neighbourhood (CEAS 1981).

Considering that these are collective problems, it might be expected that the corresponding demands and complaints would also be expressed collectively, especially given the necessary maturation time for ideas to develop into action, or from the moment of perceiving what is lacking to that of demanding solutions from the state as a citizen's right. The history of women in movements has yet to be told. From the beginning, however, involvement and/or participation by women in the more formally organized groups was certainly difficult – still more difficult in certain places and circumstances.

Women's first battles were still fought at home, against their spouses, to conquer the right to 'go out' to meetings of neighbourhood groups and associations. In these confrontations, more assertive women prevail in the battles: they end up joining and often staying in the group. Others, however, eventually give up, or start to participate only at a later phase after the group and its activities have acquired greater acceptance and legitimacy.

As women who participated in some of the earlier movements confide:

> There are some [husbands] who do not like it at all. There are even some who forbid their wives to come to the meetings. In our group, at least, there

was a woman who told us that her husband did not want her to participate any more because she was getting to be smarter than he (CEAS 1978).

There are husbands who beat up their wives when they start to come to the meetings. These husbands think just like their bosses (CEAS 1981).

Here in our neighbourhood there is a girl who helps us a lot in our meetings. She broke her engagement when the guy demanded that she stop participating in our meetings (CEAS 1981).

Of course, there are noted exceptions to this type of behaviour, revealed in testimonies such as this:

While there are some women who come behind their husbands' backs, there are others whose husbands tell them to participate. Because he already heard his wife talking about 'assemblies', 'women's day', and the like. Then, he puffs up with pride, noting that his wife is growing and that she is being noticed by others (CEAS 1978).

Half-way between their traditional roles and learning new social behaviours in the public domain, women of the working class find still other difficulties or initial barriers (besides the family-related ones) which through their efforts are gradually being overcome. These difficulties are primarily related to their lack of practical knowledge, outside the home, as well as to the traditional social devaluation of their experiences and know-how, which are usually focused on customary family life. Furthermore, their male comrades in the movements always expect them to take charge of the supposedly more 'feminine' tasks in the group. The existent prejudices against women who lead a more independent life also merit mention (Filgueiras 1984; Caldeira 1990).

It is important to call attention to the presence of 'intermediaries', or external social agents, in these movements and, in particular, to the Catholic Church's influence in many grassroots groups in facilitating, if not initiating, the mobilization of women. Either by inviting reluctant women to join existing groups, or by creating new ones, the Church played an instrumental role. Mother's clubs (*Clubes de Mães*), for example, often developed into discussion groups on gender-related issues, or laid the basis for some of the emerging urban social movements struggling for better health care services and the like. In many instances, simply by providing space – and relatively 'sacred space' – for meetings and group activities, the Church granted groups legitimacy, particularly because it has always been regarded as 'natural' for women to be involved in Church activities (even if only in cleaning and maintaining the church, or caring for the pastor's liturgical apparel).

Some husbands even told their 'nervous' wives to join the *Clubes de Mães* just to have some fun.

New tendencies in gender relations can be detected in women's testimonies, such as that of a member of the directing council of a neighbourhood association in Salvador this past year. According to her, when she first joined the association her husband stood against her involvement; but she did not give up. As time wore on and her work began to yield results, he started to stay at home and care for the children while she went out to the meetings and took part in the activities. Eventually, he also assumed responsibility for cooking the meals whenever his working hours allowed. 'He is a lousy cook,' she jokingly admitted.

Other testimonies also reveal possibilities for the establishment of new patterns of gender relations:

> The president of the association, for instance, changed a lot. His wife gave us her version. He is no longer a *machão* (a 'male chauvinist pig'). Other men also have changed.

> When we had a meeting of all the members in Mar Grande, we took turns in doing the domestic chores. Some men did not want to take their turn, some complained they did not know how to do them. And some women felt constrained: with so many women around, to put the men in the kitchen! But they all had to learn (CEAS 1981).

WOMEN AS LEADERS

Nowadays, the participation of women in neighbourhood movements is totally secure. Long past is the time, described by Cardoso (1983) in a pioneering work, when women were called upon to join and even lead the movements because, not being political actors, they could 'afford to lose'; and gone is the time when women 'sustained' the doubtful beginnings of a movement, passing the leadership on to men when the movement became successful.

Today, one finds several powerful female leaders heading many neighbourhood associations. In Salvador, for instance, a recent study has already disclosed that 42 per cent of the presidents of the neighbourhood associations interviewed thus far are women (Espineira 1990).

Retracing the trajectories of different struggles and of the leaders involved, one finds that these women are still identified with a motherly image – though now they are seen as powerful, collective mothers. As women often say: 'in *my* association this is not done'; 'in *my* commission, I want it this way. . . .' Moreover, this new image of power, identified with women – an image still being formed through daily lives and struggles of the poor neighborhoods throughout Brazil – is actually none other than those imprecise images springing from the past, from the ever-present underlying domestic power of women. This is a matter still little discussed, and understood even less.

Conscious of the worth of their militancy and actions, many women have gone so far as to make over-exultant claims regarding gender relations. In comparing women's and men's performances in these neighbourhood movements, for example, one woman stated:

> Personally, I have nothing against men. But it is often the women who have the courage to take action when faced with the garbage on the streets, the lack of basic sanitation....

> It is not because of their jobs. Many of them [the men] are unemployed. But they prefer to play dominoes instead.

> Nowadays, in our association, there are many more men. But not at first: then it was only women. Men started to approach slowly when they saw the concrete results of the actions of women (CEAS 1981).

Of course, the process of social growth and concern does not reach all women with the same intensity, or at the same pace. There are certainly blatant differences between the rather avant-garde attitudes of the leaders and the slower pace of their followers. Differences in the perspectives and disposition of women of different generations can also be expected.

While discussing the 'newness' of the neighbourhood associations for residents in different areas of Salvador, Moura (1990) had this to say about discrepant attitudes between the leadership and the other participants:

> The leaders are often seen as somewhat external agents, since they interfere in the 'normal life' of the *invasão* by means of elements assimilated elsewhere. Some envy the leaders, because of their ease in talking about uncommon matters as well as in promoting different activities. But this can also be interpreted as a lack of respect for the existing social order to which the residents have grown accustomed and the very order which provides the basis of their self-identification.

But even the non-leader women perceive their personal gains in being involved in the movements, as revealed in a testimony recorded by the same author:

> I used to be an ignorant woman. Really ignorant. I knew nothing. Now I can speak up about what I think. I know how to talk, and what I think I am capable of doing I do. At the beginning, I was really embarrassed, but I

have outgrown it by now, thank goodness. I am a new woman.

Her attitudes and feelings are similar to those expressed by a domestic servant, then involved in the local association of domestic workers, when referring to her experiences: 'I am still sort of nervous, but now I go out and speak up' (Britto Da Motta 1987).

One of the more notable results of the successful mobilization of women on the basis of their family roles in turn aiding the emergence of a 'public' maternality, and contributing to turning the 'private' into 'public' – is the political and social recognition of the public face of reproduction. This shift, as Jelin (1990) appropriately notes, 'removes from women part of the load and responsibility (with a measure of guilt) for the conditions in which the family is maintained'.

It is also important to note that the more active women have been gradually broadening the scope of their involvement. Multi-militancy, or the simultaneous activism of women in different social movements, is currently a commonly observed practice. Likewise, a trend is evident towards the opening up of the spatial boundaries of women's involvement: from neighbourhoods to city and state-wide arenas, from associations to federations, and from there to confederations.... The path traced by Benedita da Silva – a black, formerly poor woman, an ex-domestic servant, resident of one of Rio's *favelas*, who worked her way through neighbourhood struggles into the City Council and, from there, to a seat in the National Congress, where she played a key role in discussions that preceded the formulation of the constitution – is certainly a case in point.

Overall, it is women's 'getting out of the house', of course, that is *really* the novelty. No doubt, some women as individuals have always done this: but now there are significant numbers of women, particularly those of low education levels, involved in political activities and thus in the 'public' domain. This is so new, in fact, that most of the women themselves have yet to perceive that they are actually involved in 'politics' (Caldeira 1990).

Moreover, women's 'getting out of the house', coupled with men's gradual involvement in domestic activities – and a lot of solidarity-building between them in the meantime – may in fact have enormous consequences at both individual and social levels of experience, thus presenting new problems for social analysis and theory builders so far addressed by only a handful of women: Souza Lobo (1987), Safa (1989), Jelin (1990), Caldeira (1990), Alvarez (1990).

The Public Identity of Women: New Consciousness, New Image

Among the different consequences of these processes, two seem fundamental to us: one is the ensuing construction of a new collective
consciousness of gender, developed in day-to-day meetings and neighbourhood struggles, particularly as women face one another as women,
in comparison to men, and become aware of their subordinated condition as well as of their potential for change. The other pertains to the
construction of a new image 'of women as social actors in public
domains', which, as Souza Lobo (1987) observes, is still developing 'in
an ambiguous but meaningful way'.

These two different, yet related, processes actually draw attention to
two gigantic leaps yet to be taken. On the one hand, the collective
construction of a consciousness of gender opens the possibility for
women to surpass their fragmented identity, now only partially visible
and then only through the screen of the mother/wife role. On the other
hand, the constitution of a 'new' political image for women will eventually lead to a fading of the lines of separation between the 'public' and
'private' spheres, which in turn will foster women's thorough questioning of existing gender hierarchies. All this may lead to women and men
alike rethinking their roles and domains in society.

Notes

1. This article was written in 1990, when Fernando Collor was the President
   of Brazil. Under Collor's successor, Itamar Franco, these policies have not
   changed substantially in regard to the living conditions of the working
   classes.
2. It is evident that this increase is not due only to working-class women's
   greater involvement in the market, nor can we explain their involvement
   solely in terms of the process of pauperization of the labouring classes.
   Besides, new job opportunities for women have been much more directed
   to middle-class women, mainly those of higher education levels, who
   actually account for a considerable proportion of the noted rate increases.
   On the other hand, the growth of the female labour force results from the
   combination of a series of different factors, among which we may cite:
   changes in the productive structure specific to an economy which becomes
   predominantly urban; specific dynamics of some sectors and/or occupa-

tions; and, finally, changing attitudes regarding women's roles, resulting from changes in the ideological basis of the sexual division of labour and corresponding symbolic representations, which reflect, in part, the influence of the contemporary feminist movement.
3. It should be noted that membership of political parties is actually rather low in Brazil, regardless of sex. According to the 1988 PNAD data, for instance, only 2.6 per cent of all Brazilians are officially affiliated to political parties.
4. Including many left-wing militants and leaders who were forced to seek the help of the Catholic Church in trying to escape from the military regime's brutal persecution and repressive apparatus; and also, as a means of maintaining more direct contact with the masses, after the process of self-criticism among the so-called 'revolutionary parties', particularly of their 'vanguard' actions and practices, showed them to have become isolated from the masses.
5. Social movements in Brazil vary significantly in terms of their specific characteristics, goals and underlying ideologies. Obviously, those which have a more popular basis, such as the ones we have been discussing, are predominantly geared towards material improvements. But there are others which are directed towards denouncing specific problems, such as the Movement Against the Rising Cost of Living which drew more than one million supporting signatures on a document which was addressed and presented to governmental officials during the years of the military regime. Finally, there are also those movements which have a more symbolic-expressive character, such as the feminist and ecological movements, which are geared towards denouncing and/or modifying existing social values, attitudes and behaviour and have a greater impact among the middle class.

Bibliography

Alvarez, Sonia E. (1990). *Engendering Democracy in Brazil: Women's Movements in Transition Politics.* Princeton, New Jersey: Princeton University Press.
Arroyo, Raimundo (1978). 'Empobrecimento relativo e absoluto do proletariado brasileiro na última década'. In Arroyo, *A situação da classe trabalhadora na América.* Rio de Janeiro: Paz e Terra.
Britto Da Motta, Alda (1977). 'Visão do Mundo da Empregada Doméstica'. Master's thesis, Universidade Federal da Bahia, Mestrado em Ciências Humanas.
Britto Da Motta, Alda (1987). 'Associations of domestic servants – the case of Bahia, Brazil'. Paper presented at the Third International Interdisciplinary Congress on Women, Trinity College, Dublin.
Britto Da Motta, Alda (1990). *Relações de gênero em movimentos de bairro no subúrbio de Salvador.* Research in progress. NEIM/UFBa.

Caldeira, Tereza Pires do Rio (1984). *A política dos outros*. São Paulo: Brasiliense.

Caldeira, Tereza Pires do Rio (1990). 'Women, daily life and politics'. In E. Jelin (ed.), *Women and Social Change in Latin America*. London: UNRISD/Zed Books.

Camargo, Aspàsia and Diniz, Eli (eds) (1989). *Continuidade e mudança no Brasil da Nova República*. São Paulo: Vértice/Ed. Revista dos Tribunais.

Cardoso, Ruth (1983). 'Movimentos sociais urbanos: balanço crítico'. In: B. Sorj and M. H. Almeida (eds), *Sociedade e política no Brasil Pós-64*. São Paulo: Brasiliense.

Carvalho, Inaiá Maria Moreira de (1984). 'Pauperização e condições de subsistência de trabalhadores urbanos'. In Carvalho, I. and Haguette, T. M. (eds), *Trábalho e condições de vida no nordeste brasileiro*. São Paulo/Brasília: Hucitec/CNPq.

Carvalho, Inaiá Maria Moreira de (1987). 'Urbanização, mercado de trabalho e pauperização no nordeste brasileiro. Uma resenha de estudos recentes'. *BIB*, 22 Rio de Janeiro: ANPOCS.

Carvalho, Inaiá Maria Moreira de and Laniado, Ruthy Nadia (1990). 'Movimentos sociais e democracia: novos fatos em busca de uma teorização'. *Caderno CRH,* 13 (July– December). Salvador, Bahia: CRH/UFBA and Ed. Fator.

CEAS (1978). 'A luta das mães por um Brasil melhor'. *Cadernos do CEAS,* 58 (November/December). Salvador, Bahia.

CEAS (1981). 'Mulheres da periferia com a palavra'. *Cadernos do CEAS,* 74, (July/August). Salvador, Bahia.

Durhan, Eunice (1984). 'Movimentos sociais: a construção da cidadania'. *Novos Estudos CEBRAP*, 10. São Paulo: CEBRAP.

Espiñeira, Victoria Gonzalez (1990). 'Movimentos de bairro: o comunista, a Igreja e o Estado. Projeto de pesquisa visando dissertação de Mestrado'. Mestrado em Ciências Sociais, UFBa.

Filgueiras, Cristina (1984). 'Participação das mulheres na organização dos moradores do bairro da Água Branca'. Paper presented at the VIII Annual meeting of ANPOCS. Águas de São Pedro: São Paulo.

Fundação Instituto Brasileiro de Geografia e Estatóstica (IBGE) (1990). 'Participação político-social, 1988'. Rio de Janeiro: IBGE (PNAD, 1 and 2).

Jelin, Elizabeth (1990). 'Introduction'. In Jelin, Elizabeth (ed.), *Women and Social Change in Latin America*. London: UNRISD/Zed Books.

Kergoat, Danièle (1978). 'Ouvriers = ouvrières? (Propositions pour une articulation théorique de deux variables: sexe et classe sociale)'. *Critiques de l'Economie Politique,* 5 (October/December).

Moura, Alexandrina Sobreira de (ed.) (1989). *O Estado e as políticas públicas na transição democrática*. São Paulo/Recife: Vértice/Ed. Revista dos Tribunais.

Moura, Milton (1990). 'A participação política no meio de baixa renda (uma reflexão a partir do movimento de moradores de Salvador)'. *Cadernos do CEAS,* 130 (November/December).

O'Donnell, Guillermo (1982). 'Tensões do Estado autoritário burocrático e a questão da América Latina'. In D. Collier (ed.), *O novo autoritarismo na América Latina*. Rio de Janeiro: Paz e Terra.

Safa, Helen I. (1989). 'Towards a theory of women's collective action in Latin America'. Florida: Centre for Latin American Studies, University of Florida. Mimeo.

Souto-Maior, Haroldo (1990). 'Renda familiar no nordeste: 1970–1987'. In *Anais do VII Encontro Nacional de Estudos Populacionais*, Vol. 1. São Paulo: ABEP.

Souza Lobo, Elizabeth (1987). 'Homem e mulher: imagens nas Ciências Sociais'. ANPOCS/CNDM.

6

DEVELOPMENT AND ECONOMIC CRISIS: WOMEN'S LABOUR AND SOCIAL POLICIES IN VENEZUELA IN THE CONTEXT OF INTERNATIONAL INDEBTEDNESS

Giovanna Franca Dalla Costa

Venezuela in the 1970s: the Leap that Failed

In the second half of the 1970s under Carlos Andrés Pérez's first presidency, Venezuela entered a phase characterized by a striking level of import substitution, coupled with a resumption of the interplay between private and public capital and, above all, the emergence of a series of new features in domestic capital's role and importance with respect to foreign capital. It was a time when the state intervened more directly in the economy, strengthening its entrepreneurial commitment with the declared intention of building a 'national path' to development, designed to achieve less extensive dependence on the industrial countries. To a large degree, the new economic choices were to be supported by resources from a public budget that had grown significantly thanks to increased oil and raw materials prices.

In this phase, growth in Venezuela had many aspects in common with what was happening in those same years in other Third World oil-producing states, above all a search for greater independence in national economic policy and, at the same time, a review of development criteria in an attempt to limit the extent to which the industrial countries could impose their will. One factor was certainly the heavy pressures from the local intermediate entrepreneurial and professional classes, who were demanding a more substantial participation in the profits from the production and sale of oil.

In Venezuela, the leap in production was made under the aegis of a nationalization that sanctioned the state's hegemony in the crucial sectors of the country's economic and industrial structure, imposing a strong reduction in the role of foreign capital. Nationalization was applied in sectors reckoned to be strategic for the economy's 'emancipation'. It was laid down that foreign capital, albeit in return for heavy indemnities, would be subject to precise limits, particularly as regards the reinvestment of profits within the country. Placed in the national system of public sector enterprises, we find sectors such as oil, petrochemicals and metallurgy, finance, electrical energy, transport and telecommunications, manufacturing and agro-industry, shipbuilding, mining, and tourism (Equipo Proceso Politico 1978: 55).

Yet, private capital played a very important function, too, since it was located in highly profitable areas of the economy, particularly those addressed to the domestic market and in large part guaranteed by public investment (Equipo Proceso Politico 1978: 49). (Suffice it to cite the housing sector, in which a strengthened private entrepreneurship found a favourable terrain in governmental low-cost housing programmes for the local people; the same can be said for home furnishings and clothing, where there was also space for the affirmation of private business in the shadow of government projects.) More generally, within the framework of the nationalization programme, no statutory limits were placed on private capital as regards activities not linked to the basic productive processes, while in those that were so linked, different conditions of participation were established according to the category of production. In the petrochemical sector for primary products, for example, only public capital was admitted; for derived products, private capital was granted a stake of up to 49 per cent; for complementary products, private capital was granted the possibility of a majority stake (Equipo Proceso Politico 1978: 48).

Nationalization was justified in strongly demagogic tones as a great economic, political and social revolution capable of freeing the state from the 'imperialist yoke', said by the government to be responsible for eroding the country's wealth and creating the population's impoverishment. Above all, in the initial period of the first Pérez presidency, the direct involvement of government and president in creating and propagating initiatives for the country's productive development was enormous.

Public intervention was everywhere accompanied by important supporting actions and campaigns, conducted not only under the president's aegis, but also with his direct commitment, with the aim of reawakening working fervour and discipline in the people. The new course of production, then, went in step with a considerable and, in certain ways, novel involvement of political power, in educational and cultural terms as well, with a commitment that tried to convey the economic project's social scope and its potential redistributive function in favour of the popular masses (Malavé Mata 1987).

On the other hand, this was certainly the only option. Traditionally, there was a void between the government and a people who had little familiarity with any structured and consolidated form of individual and collective discipline, who were massively extraneous to citizenship norms, and who were impermeable to identification with and participation in public programmes. The roots of this mass extraneousness to government policy ran deep, and had vast implications – certainly more than one might imagine from popular protest against the government. The protest was there, of course, but in those years it was not particularly extended or effective. They were years of relative social peace in which the left-wing forces contained their clashes with the government within narrow limits.

The bargaining potential offered by the economic turn-around in terms of improved international conditions of development and a different domestic distribution of resources and income was wasted in a big way. Nationalization ended as a transitory readjustment of the relationship between national bourgeoisie and transnational bourgeoisie, against a background of increased state finance (Petras and Morley 1983). For some years, the professional, industrial and commercial middle classes would simply enjoy greater influence and more ample margins in their economic operations by exercising strong pressures on the state to obtain a more substantial participation in profits and for a direct control over policy.

In any case, within this framework, substantial differences between the state and the entrepreneurs were quick to emerge over the nature and form of the investments to be made. This problematic relationship led quickly to a proliferation of wealthy bureaucrats and runaway corruption, which contributed to accelerating the development plan's failure (Malavé Mata 1987). On one hand, in fact, the new dynamism and efficiency found in the Venezuelan economy as a whole as it sought higher productivity meant creating a more homogeneous set of rules for public- and private-sector businesses – and, significantly enough, wage norms in the two sectors were also made more homogeneous (Ley general 1979).

On the other hand, there could be no convergence between the two sectors' development requirements. The state had large amounts of capital in areas where profit rates were not always especially high (including aluminium) and the level of competitivity was low compared to some sectors of private industry. The long-term industrial development plans – for example, Plan Quatro for the development of the steel industry in the Orinoco area – were the fundamental axis for economic growth as far as the state was concerned, yet by their very nature they required a series of wide-ranging social projects which private capital was unwilling to fund. For the state, it became indispensable to strengthen the domestic market in order to absorb production, guarantee strong new external demand for the new products, and – the fundamental point – apply more effective controls on the foreign trade account in order to limit inflation and contain domestic instability.

Private capital found little to attract it to long-term industrial investments, preferring sectors with higher short-term profits, including housing and import–export trading in luxuries. The market consisted of the local bourgeoisie, an élite of consumers who had at this time acquired a very high purchasing power. But rather than the hoped-for increase in exports, the ruling productive and commercial orientations led to an unrestrained increase in imports, which finished by guiding investments into sectors that did nothing to strengthen the country's industrial structure or to create jobs in any significant way. Much investment was made abroad, and the whole operation, inside and outside the country, was conducted using the financial cover of the state.

The result is almost obvious. The state's finances rapidly dried up, while the debts contracted abroad to finance the long-term development plans and balance-of-payments disequilibriums suffocated the economy. At the same time, as the world crisis bit deeper, the international market failed to absorb the goods produced. (Exports to the Caribbean and the Andine Pact countries were a fundamental premise for productive restructuring, but they required a generalized economic growth that failed to materialize in the area.) The end of the 1970s arrived with galloping inflation and big cuts in investment plans at the major industrial complexes. Some industrial cities simply collapsed, including Puerto Ordaz, Valencia, and Barquisimeto, which had received large public funding and were the site of important initiatives by private entrepreneurs. Inflationary pressure rose to high levels.

If the 1970s ever offered Venezuela an historic chance, it was undoubtedly lost. The state's Operation Development to achieve stronger industrial take-off and more direct involvement by the public institutions soon revealed the relative insubstantiality of its economic and social foundations. Rather, policy in those years worked more as a form of redistributive 'adjustment' of wealth gained from oil and raw materials between the national and transnational bourgeoisie, with the substantial exclusion of the domestic proletariat from access to a greater share of resources.

Social Programmes of the Entrepreneurial State

What remains particularly interesting for an analysis of the state and its hypotheses on development in those years is the new commitment shown by public structures in the social sphere, which, even though it did not receive adequate attention in the socio-political analyses of the period, emerges clearly as a support for the new economic policy.

Foreseeing a widespread rise in the population's rate of reproduction, the state sought to build up at least some of the basic supports of a human capital capable of dealing with the commitment required by the new economic projects. First of all, the operation required more detailed and extensive data to replace the hitherto very partial and approximate knowledge of reproductive structures. New funds were allotted for more ample and complete social surveys, for more sophisticated research tools, and to create new specialized bodies. Research objectives became much more ambitious; the Proyecto Venezuela was conducted with the idea of measuring each and every one of the population's social and physical characteristics, a national fertility survey was made as part of the World Fertility Survey, and greater focus was achieved in related analyses.

The most urgent problem that President Pérez's V Plan for industrial and productive take-off had to face in the second half of the 1970s was the creation of a national working class. This did not necessarily need to be all that large, but it certainly had to be more efficient as labour, adequately trained as a function of the new productive tasks, and partially requalified in view of the progressive substitution of immigrant technicians. Above all, the plan had to cope with redefining the national proletariat's subsistence conditions as a whole, when most of the proletariat was unable even to ensure its own physical reproduction, yet was supposed to be able to supply replacement labour power within the more advanced conditions of production (G. F. Dalla Costa 1980, 1989a). This is the key to interpreting the striking growth in social programmes designed to enable the Venezuelan proletariat to overcome its total inadequacy to the new situation. In the 1970s, the proletarians were mostly still living in improvised homes in the urban belts and suffered heavy malnutrition and under-nutrition, with grave endemic diseases, a high frequency of mental handicap, and high illiteracy (Chossudovsky 1977; Relemberg, Karner and Koler 1979). For further and more extensive analyses of the physical and psychological picture, we refer the reader to other studies (G. F. Dalla Costa 1980, 1985, 1989a).

Yet what we have already said is enough to document the objective impossibility of incorporating the local population into productive structures and services typical of more advanced development. Of crucial importance, and widespread even outside the proletariat, was the absolute lack of training for the discipline imposed by the fundamental rules for living required in a phase of more advanced industrialization. The overwhelming majority of the population lived from its very early years in a total absence of reproductive infrastructures, starting with a basic instability in the family nucleus and, with it, in the codification of life relations, norms and styles. The basis for reproduction was not a family institutionalized in marriage, but a free union/cohabitation with a continual turnover of partners, and without sufficient income to guarantee the maintenance of the various members, whence the very frequent abandonment of minors.

In this sense, marital-paternal authority deprived of adequate material support often found no other form of 'legitimation' than violence against the women and children. The organization of the family's sexual life, which forms the necessary foundation for the organization of family and social roles, was in fact unsanctioned. Rape and incest were very frequent (the children involved were often not biological children) and, within the fabric of family life, were accompanied by other forms of 'sexual indiscipline'. Prostitution was very widespread and practised – above all – without any clear division from the family; in Venezuela, as in many other Third World countries, this became one of the mother's most important sources of income to maintain her children.

In the *barrios* (proletarian neighbourhoods) of the metropolises, the key figure in the family was the mother, who was the only real reference point, while the father was an inconstant and unpredictable figure. From the very early years, children sped through the stages of independence from their parents and soon found precarious forms of employment. As a general rule, family and social roles in Venezuela were not the channels through which political and productive control was exerted on reproduction, nor were they channels through which the social fabric could be rewoven according to the needs of that particular phase of development (G. F. Dalla Costa 1980, 1985, 1989a).

Under the pressure of productive and political necessities it had previously not been required to manage directly, the Venezuelan government, then, looked at this lack of a functional relationship between state and reproduction with new attention in the 1970s. Even if within the limits set by social expenditure that was increasing more slowly during the second half of the 1970s, the 'entrepreneurial state' was nevertheless obliged to pay a new and very careful attention to the population's reproductive style. There was a more advanced and more incisive approach towards the family, health, education, nutrition, mental health, safeguards for children, and prostitution. You no longer find enormous and indiscriminate funding – often from foreign institutions, as in the case of the family planning services run by the Ford Foundation – little of which in fact reached its intended destination. Rather, during the V Plan, there were stricter financial controls, and the funding was effected, above all, through state structures such as ministries (G. F. Dalla Costa 1980, 1985, 1989a).

CHILD CARE

To this end, new bodies were created, while others were developed by making them more specialized and coordinating them better. Near the top of the list, among child protection initiatives for the *barrios*, we find, in 1976, the relaunching of the Fundación del Niño which was given responsibility for the Hogares de cuidado diario, the Families for Day Care programme by which the children of working-class mothers were guaranteed day care in the homes of housewives for a very modest fee (Fundación del Niño 1976). Nutritional protection and education were developed, with the free distribution of food in schools and to families and education in new nutrition criteria for the population. The programmes were in large part coordinated by the Instituto Nacional de Nutrición which, as the standard-bearer of the population's physical reconstitution, proposed breast feeding in the early months (Instituto Nacional de Nutrición). In 1974, the family planning service unit, the División de Población, which had almost disappeared, resumed its activities and, in 1975, in response to International Women's Year, was placed under state control (Ministerio de Sanidad y Asistencia Social 1976).

THE FAMILY

There were also important government moves to promote responsible fatherhood. These converged from various directions in seeking to unify and consolidate the overall fatherhood role with its range of social duties and rights in the figure of the biological father. The Ministerio de la Juventud was created to promote activities addressed to young people, who represented a reality of enormous political importance: in Venezuela in the years under consideration, 60 per cent of the inhabitants were 18 or under and formed an overwhelming majority of the population (Cisor 1973, 1976). Coordinated through the Prevención del Delito programmes, these activities sought to set up barriers against diffuse juvenile delinquency by seeking to encourage a general re-orientation of lifestyles (Ministerio de Justicia 1976). Significant impetus was given to the Comisión Femenina Asesora de la Presidencia de la Republica, which would then become the Ministerio de la Mujer, as the key institution for social policies, to promote and coordinate all the programmes for women, both those designed to give her clearer responsibilities in the family and those whose aim was to provide her with new safeguards as a worker outside the family (Despacho del Ministro de Estado 1979). In appropriate government courses in both urban and rural contexts, women were thus urged to re-educate themselves as housewife-wife-mother and as waged workers. They were taught to combine housework and external work more effectively, since their traditional approach to both forms of employment was casual and precarious, because of the limited means of subsistence, in one case, and the discontinuity of paid labour in the other.

EDUCATION

Even if late in the day, the Ministerio de la Inteligencia was also created, with the assumption that policies should aim for an increase in the population's intellectual faculties through 'scientific programmes' in part borrowed from the industrial countries – for example, the Intellegentia programme put into effect in cooperation with Harvard University and with the support of the Petroleos de Venezuela oil company, the Ajedrez (Chess) programme for the development of abstract intelligence, the Fuerza Armadas programme, etc. There was also a development of the División de Venereologia del Ministerio de Sanidad y Asistencia Social for the control of prostitution, officially by carrying out medical inspections in order to cope with the increasingly widespread venereal diseases, but with the wider aim of putting a check on prostitution's uncontainable spread and the related illegal conduct (Ministerio de Justicia 1977). Finally, new units were developed for political and social action in the more distant *indios* areas where the population had previously not even been included in the census.

Certainly, Venezuela in the 1970s is an appropriate case study for tracing the new trends in reproduction policy at a time when oil wealth was plentiful and a social fabric classified as 'backward' in terms of social reproduction was creating special difficulties for social control, both because of the amplitude of the means and measures required, and because of the need to create a new institutional framework in an attempt to re-shape the social fabric more adequately to the needs of production.

INDEPENDENCE OF VENEZUELAN WOMEN

One particularly problematic aspect of these policies was certainly specific to Venezuela and not generalizable to other development contexts: the Venezuelan woman's lack of submissiveness, in her role as the family's or union's central figure, to the dictates, roles and responsibilities that the new social policies tended to assign to her (G. F. Dalla Costa 1980, 1985, 1989a). Yet, at the same time, as in other developing areas, and in some more advanced ones as well, the state's attempts to transform a substantial part of the working class were necessarily based on a redefinition of the woman's image and reproductive tasks. In the Venezuela of the 1970s, this was to prove a particularly arduous task.

It was in fact very difficult to discourage Venezuelan women from the forms of autonomy and independence that had made them somewhat unique in the panorama of Latin American images of woman. The Venezuelan family's mother-centredness, for all its repercussions on the formation of the individual and on population structure, was – and still is – a difficult obstacle in the path of the agencies and bodies charged with redefining and applying social policies.

In any case, the social policies described above were undoubtedly important precursors of the reform of reproduction and its context that was to take shape in the 1980s. This reform would centre largely on a codification of women's rights and duties and, in Venezuela in the 1980s, as in other developing countries, would form the fundamental axis for capitalist restructuring – a reform that these countries would maintain, even when the IMF's squeeze required them to cut their social expenditure so drastically as to prejudice the survival of the population's poorer strata.

Economic Crisis and Indebtedness

Many social scientists agree that an appropriate target for Venezuela to achieve by the year 2000 is now the standard of living it had in 1980; that the promotion of basic education has become such a major goal as to require a substantial renewal of the political system if it is to be achieved; that it is unthinkable to guarantee institutional democracy while leaving aside all democratic inspiration in social policies. The picture is such as to cast serious doubt on the utility of planning (Silva Michelena 1987: 24).

This, at least, was the consideration with which the great social scientist, the late José A. Silva Michelena, interpreting the views of the various scholars taking part, introduced 'Coloquio: Venezuela hacia el año 2000', a seminar organized in November 1986 to assess the country's national and international future until the year 2000.

In effect, the crisis of the 1980s very quickly gobbled up the small advances made in Venezuela in previous decades, as regards both the country's economic and work structure and its social policies, both of which had had some positive, even if always minimal effects on the population's living standards. The *salto atràs* (backward leap) was so brutal and sudden that the few conquests that seemed permanent, including a falling trend in endemic diseases and child mortality, melted away to give place to the sores of a body that one realized had never been cured. The body of society was disfigured and dying, supine between the lack of material means for subsistence, the violence of an increasingly extended and far-reaching repression, and the riskiness of a daily life increasingly invaded by criminal gangs of various origins settling their accounts. As the 1990s dawned, the diseased and desperate body of society was forced down into the streets to win its bread. The recession was the deepest Venezuela had seen in the current century.

It certainly needs no repeating that throughout the 1980s the most decisive problem for Latin America, and the developing countries in general, was the foreign debt – dramatic testimony to the contradictions characterizing a form of a development whose whole thrust was against the Third World. José A. Silva Michelena quantified the scale of the debt in 1987, and offered a forecast for 2000:

> Since the crisis in 1982 when Mexico threatened to stop making its payments, [the debt] has grown by 26 per cent to reach the frightening figure of $1,015 billion. Almost half of this is owed by Latin America. Thanks to this, the Latin American continent has become a financier of the developed countries. In effect, the transfer of capital for debt servicing reached $140 billion dollars between 1982 and 1986. Continuing at this rate, Latin America will have transferred a further $400 billion in the 13 years remaining to the year 2000. If you add in transfers due to the flight of capital, the deterioration in the terms of trade, and illegal trafficking in arms and drugs, the total for the end of the century can be estimated at over $1,000 billion, or as much as the whole Third World debt. This is a bleeding white without parallel in history (J. A. Silva Michelena 1987: 25–6).

The developing countries' debts must be considered in parallel with the world economy's great transformations, whether structural or not, until the end of the century. Fundamentally, one sees a split between financial and real economy, an unfavourable relationship between industrial production and employment, a widening gap between welfare conditions in the developed areas and the trend in the underdeveloped ones, and a deep influence of technology in which the Third World is strongly penalized in terms of finance and destination: only 1 per cent of finance devoted to technological research world-wide concerns technology applicable in the Third World (Anderson 1987: 86). All these aspects have been analysed thoroughly by G. Martner (Martner 1987: 47–80), and they are summed up as follows by J. A. Michelena.

> Financial activities have gotten detached from the real economy. To make the point, it is enough to recall that, while the real economy tops $3,000 billion, financial activities top $75 trillion [T, d.A.] (J. A. Silva Michelena: 1987: 26).

> Another characteristic of the world economy is the split between industrial production and employment. This is a long-term trend which represents capitalism's greatest historical challenge.... There is also a split between growth in the developed and underdeveloped countries. North–South relations tend to acquire increasing importance, while demand for the underdeveloped countries' typical products (raw materials) is falling. As the value of resources created by men is enhanced, so raw materials lose their value. Latin America, for example, has lost importance in the world economy relatively speaking (J. A. Silva Michelena 1987: 27).

Undoubtedly, this trend

> is strengthened by the substitution effects created by rapid technological changes, and these determine a rapid deterioration of the terms of trade (J. A. Silva Michelena 1987: 27).

THE OIL ECONOMY

The international situation, then, is a daunting one in which Venezuela, although an oil producer, has few means for intervention. In fact, even though oil will continue to maintain its importance because of the limited development of alternative energy sources, world economic growth trends show a proportionally lower need for energy, leaving Venezuela with very limited margins for manoeuvre. According to the estimates of A. Quirós Corradi (Quirós Corradi 1987: 81–124) illustrated in J. A. Silva Michelena's introduction,

> the oil economy depends on a series of international factors over which Venezuela can exercise very little or no influence. Whence, leaving aside the fact that with respect to oil the only safe prediction is that 'predictions cannot be made', an effort must be made to assess the trend of these factors....

> We have already seen that the growth of the world economy until the year 2000 will not be spectacular and, as if that were not enough, one can expect

that the relationship between economic growth and demand for energy, which was 1–to–1 until recently, will continue to fall below the ratio of 1–to–0.6 at which it now stands....

Other energy sources will enjoy limited development, whence one can expect oil to increase its importance, rising from 49.8 million barrels in 1990 to 52.6 million in the year 2000. Given OPEC's policy, one can theorize that production will lie between 20 and 23 million barrels in 1990, rising gradually to 25-29 million in the year 2000 (J. A. Silva Michelena 1987: 28).

One can also theorize that energy saving efforts will continue despite growing costs, since there is a very determined awareness as regards the need to produce more with less energy (J. A. Silva Michelena 1987: 29).

Again using A. Quirós's figures, in consideration of all these factors, future oil prices can be analysed according to two scenarios, one with prices below $25 per barrel in 1995 and $45 in 2000, the second with prices above $30 in 1995 and $55 in 2000, the difference between the two cases being decisive for whether or not the Venezuelan oil industry can continue financing its own needs (J. A. Silva Michelena 1987: 29).

In any case, the Venezuelan economy certainly seems likely to continue being an oil-based one for a long time to come, a conclusion that also implies a high level of unpredictability with respect to the country's international economic and political future. To succeed in controlling the more important economic and political consequences of having an oil-based economy, one of the greatest challenges seems to be to manage to

diversify and strengthen the sources of fiscal and currency revenues, since while oil will continue to be an important source of finance, its participation in fiscal revenue will fall progressively. As to the currency contribution from the oil industry, one estimate is that ... it will maintain the [1986 level] until 1991, a year in which an important increase is expected. In 1995, another increase is seen as possible, then gradual growth until 2000. Given these figures, there is no doubt, then, that one of the most important challenges for the current government is to succeed in drawing up a global oil policy to avoid unnecessary traumas for industry and a development policy to make it possible to cope with the relative scarcity of hard currency ... (J. A. Silva Michelena 1987: 29–30).

THE NON-OIL ECONOMY

As regards the non-oil economy, while there was agreement on the need for change and diversification in the productive sectors, there seemed to

be no clarity as to what, how or when things should be done (Yañez Betancourt 1987: 125–62; Haussman 1987: 163–82). Then, with respect to a general outline for the 'reduction of disequilibriums', different ideas coexisted as to interventions and operational solutions, including the creation of a Fondo de Estabilización Macroeconomica at the Venezuelan central bank to finance the deficit by using short-term measures when oil income is low and accumulating funds when it is high (Haussmann 1987: 181).

On the other hand, the strong under-utilization of industrial plant, with 40 per cent of productive capacity in reserve, brought out double-shift solutions to optimize the use of plant at the national level (Misle 1987: 20), and also ideas for integrating wages with coupons as a way of supporting domestic demand and, hence, containing the discrepancy that would appear between productivity and real wage (Misle 1987: 23). These wage supplements would also represent a mediation with respect to the entrepreneurs' unwillingness to accept, in years of crisis, the new labour costs that the intensification of production and the extension of double-shift working would entail.

New breathing space was also given to the promotion of till then relatively neglected economic sectors which were nonetheless important channels for foreign currency revenues. Tourism, for example, was one of those that began to receive greater support.

Certainly, extensive unemployment, precariousness of jobs, and low wages will remain in Venezuela's near future, determining a scenario in which a return to the relatively high employment levels of the second half of the 1970s is no more than a distant possibility. In 1986, the unemployment rate had settled at 11 per cent, according to official sources, and at 17 per cent, according to a Gallup survey (Misle 1987: 20).

The economic and political impasse and extreme marginalization from the international market suffered in those years by Venezuela and Latin America as a whole are recognized as an established fact. According to J. C. Rey's analysis (Rey 1987: 183–246), in more strictly political terms, this marginalization was suffered within a hegemonic reaffirmation of the United States, whence this continent would seem destined to remain in these conditions

until its role in the new world economic order is well defined. This is a reason for the interventionist policy through which an attempt is being made [by the USA] to contain or liquidate experiments designed to build new models of society, as in the case of Grenada or Nicaragua, while at the same time blackmailing all countries through the debt and actions imposed by the IMF (J. A. Silva Michelena 1987: 27).

Blackmail is therefore enforced and ensures that planning remains hostage to the search for survival, so that any real economic and social strategy is almost totally abandoned.

For Venezuela, but also for all Latin America, says J. A. Silva Michelena,

> interest in medium- and long-term problems has almost disappeared, even at planning centres, and the debate is focused on specific problems whose time-scale does not extend beyond three months. Studying the factors involved in re-negotiating the debt with the international banks, exchange-rate changes, the evolution of interest rates, tariff levels, the effects of protectionism, and other similar problems seize the attention of the decision-makers and the scholars most concerned with the nation's situation. Very few dare think much beyond six months, and imagination is imprisoned by small details... Yet, there is an awareness that a lasting and structural solution, both for those specific problems and the global crisis, can only be found in the long term. The years remaining before the beginning of the twenty-first century will be crucial, in the sense that the decisions taken in this period will determine what settles into place in the next century, whence the importance of reflecting on what may happen, and what must be done in these vital 13 years remaining before 2000. Given this picture, one of the most complex intellectual challenges today is to re-think and redeem the practical Utopia of achieving survival (J. A. Silva Michelena 1987: 23–4).

From Social Intervention to Social Control

The climate of crisis encouraged paralysis, but in the debate to redefine economic policy, the paralysis could not be allowed to produce or consolidate an abyss of alienation between state and population. In the years of recession, the search for more extensive and controlled communication with the poorer strata of the population never stopped. But the framework had changed from the 1970s, when there had been the earlier attempt to acquire improved knowledge and open up channels of communication (G. F. Dalla Costa 1980, 1985, 1988, 1989a). Then, the state needed to improve its capability for social intervention so that it could achieve more adequate levels of qualification and integration in support of attempted industrial take-off during the more accentuated phase of import substitution. Now, the aims become a new relationship with the population's poorer strata and the organization of channels, instruments and other means for penetrating the body of society with a more defined 'integrated intervention system', in the search for greater support in, and greater control over, a crisis situation (G. F. Dalla Costa 1989b).

Today, the problem is to contain and monitor the political, economic and social chaos that is continually bursting to the surface of unsustainable living conditions. The streets are already a theatre for extensive bread struggles, inflation is very grave, the production and circulation of goods is almost completely dislocated, and social reproduction is increasingly reduced to simple survival strategies that are not only beyond all control, but are in many cases illegal: drug trafficking, prostitution, and other trafficking of various kinds.

A big problem for the state is to maintain some form of contact with the population and to ensure that at least some social channels remain open for old and new forms of control, in order to apply the austerity policies currently proposed as a corrective for the crisis, even though they certainly cannot pretend to supply effective social services to the have-nots. Its economic and social policy has been reduced almost to zero, but the state must nonetheless maintain some capability for 'organizing society', since that is the premise for getting out of the crisis.

> Venezuela has a way out, the resources are there. There are Venezuelans who want to work more, and there are other Venezuelans who want to consume more. The nub of the problem lies in the capacity to organize society so it can pull it off (Haussman 1987: 182).

But, in the 1980s, given the lack of outlets for employment and the heavy reduction in social welfare, the capacity for organizing society was, to say the least, compromised. The employment picture was near enough to collapse to discourage both those who wanted to work more and those who wanted to consume more. There was a shift

> from 4 per cent unemployment in 1978 to 14 per cent in 1985, while the informal sector passed in the same period from 28 per cent of urban employment to 44 per cent. Moreover, with cuts in education, health and housing services, the Venezuelan worker's capacity for production would deteriorate seriously (Haussman 1987: 176).

The population was largely without a wage, and the available jobs were precarious ones in the informal sector, even in cities where past migration in search of more lasting employment had produced heavy concentrations of proletarians. In terms of qualification, too, thanks to the cuts in basic education, health and housing services, labour power settled back to the lower levels of manual labour. This was a complete retreat from the possibilities for requalifying this type of labour power that emerged in the second half of the 1970s, after the first big leap in oil prices (G. F. Dalla Costa 1980, 1985, 1988, 1989a).

The Impact of the Crisis on Women

A very important point, and one that was crucial in Venezuela, was that the burden of the worsening labour situation fell especially heavily on the women, as regards both income levels and job openings. This had important social implications, precisely because, to a degree far greater than is found in the so-called advanced areas, the woman was the head of the family (G. F. Dalla Costa 1980, 1985, 1988, 1989a; Ministerio de la Juventud 1985a, 1985b). In the context of the Venezuelan crisis, the further impoverishment of women translated directly into worse living conditions throughout the fabric of society, since the entire organization of the population's reproduction rests more on the woman than on the couple.

'The regressiveness of income distribution in Venezuela is evident,' wrote the economist, Adicea Castillo, comparing the peak of the crisis in 1984 with the situation in 1981.

If we consider the systematic increase in retail prices ... there is no difficulty in understanding why I locate as suffering critical poverty levels all those sectors with an income equal to or less than 3.000 Bolivares. Clearly, I consider as absolutely insufficient the recently established minimum wage of 1.500 Bs for urban workers and 1.200 Bs for rural workers. Of the 71.5 per cent of clerks and workers with incomes of less than 3.000 Bs, and of the 79 per cent of self-employed workers with the same low income – basically, handworkers, salespersons, forestry workers etc. – a good number are women.

However much the number of women heading a family may show systematic growth and also find reflection in the official statistics, the women continue to be considered as a 'secondary labour reserve' and therefore receive lower wages for the same work. In many firms producing textiles, clothing, etc. and in other sectors, the productivity of the women is higher than the men's, yet the women receive lower wages.

If one analyses the indexes of women's employment in the various industries and activities, the general observation is of a clear reduction in the number of women employed in almost all sectors, especially in manufacturing where there was a fall from 28.10 per cent to 25.19 per cent. The biggest contractions ranged from 31.0 per cent to 28.18 per cent in the food, drinks and tobacco sectors; from 60.9 per cent to 53.51 per cent in textiles, clothing and leather; from 19.0 per cent to 13.64 per cent in the manufacture of non-metal mineral products ... and from 57.2 per cent to 50.1 per cent in personal services. In the case of women's labour, the already grave conditions for all workers are aggravated still more because the woman's wage is considered as a *support wage* and women are placed in the worst paid functions (A. Castillo 1985: 60).

Overall, there is nothing new under the sun in the general context of discrimination against women at work. Rather, the spotlight is cast on the gravity of the situation for women's labour in the Venezuelan crisis, a gravity that was also noted by the leading international bodies (International Labour Organization 1984).

The job situation, then, was thoroughly precarious, and especially serious for women. Yet the quality and magnitude of social assistance were reduced to very modest levels, in terms of the services offered and the financial support supplied. At the same time, the assistance was addressed only to areas of extreme need and critical poverty (Garcia 1987), and one of its main aims was the search for new and more extensive forms of social integration. As a whole, the approach was, on one hand, to discourage expectations as regards the supply of services and material resources by the state – state assistance was to be regarded as dead and buried – and, on the other, to promote new forms for the citizen's identification with the state by multiplying the pressures for participation and consensus, even among the people of the *barrios*, who traditionally had a flimsy rapport with state institutions.

Popular Resistance

Public intervention thus envisaged had to confront extensive opposition from a part, and above all the proletarian part, of the population. There was an outburst of street struggles related to primary needs, and the state was identified as the main culprit for the population's grave impoverishment and for the failure to safeguard national wealth through adequate opposition to the IMF's famine-creating paths. The whole history of colonialism returned to the limelight in this catastrophic scenario. It surfaced at all levels, starting from the roots. For, in these same years, there was social and cultural protest in the streets and the universities against the 500th anniversary celebration of the 'discovery of America'. Many declared that they would have preferred not to have been discovered, and some said that national poverty was such that there seemed to be nothing to celebrate on the day *en el cual ustedes nos descubiernos* (when you discovered us).

A total dichotomy was to be found, then, between a public intervention obedient to the IMF/World Bank dictates, and a social reality lying at the roots of an imposing escalation of violence. By this time, there were hundreds of dead in the streets, starting with those of Caracas and Merida in 1989, during the above-mentioned bread struggles (*La Repubblica*, 4 March 1989). At the same time, the organization of new forms of social control was being proposed. With government support, extensive moves were set under way in the *barrios* for 'self-management' in social control, by collecting denunciations for drug dealing, other forms of criminality, and the illegal trafficking off which the people of the *barrios*, and the women above all, traditionally live. Significantly enough, these were also the years when a debate began on a bill to extend penal responsibility to minors.

At the same time, the state sought a new legitimation through vast projects to reform and transform the institutions, committing itself to 'self-restructuring' in the midst of heavy and conflicting pressures from social forces, political parties, entrepreneurs, and various institutional sectors. The inadequacy of the state apparatus to political and economic reality and the scope and structure of society was universally recognized: 'Despite the enormous dimensions of the state apparatus, it is unable to control the growing complexity of our society' (De La Cruz 1987: 248).

Decentralization, a reduction in the state apparatus, and rationalization of the public administration (De La Cruz 1987: 265–7) were to be the axes along which this restructuring would be achieved. In them, one can find some parallels with the debate in this area in the developed states: for example, in questioning the relationship between central and peripheral power. In Venezuela, there was certainly a wide-ranging scenario of reform through which the state was supposed to cope with its now historical inadequacies with respect to possible future political and economic perspectives. The path was a tortuous one through the various alliances and resistances set up by political and economic forces linked in various ways to the centre and periphery. In this scenario, the reforms were capable of breaking up old power centres to build new ones, yet they were still far from supplying the kind of epoch-making response required by the ongoing crisis: a crisis in the development model and, hence, a crisis in the type of accumulation and the type of domination:

> that is, that at the very bottom of the current crisis of the state, there is the 'exhaustion' of the development model, which brings with it both a crisis in the type of accumulation and a crisis in the ruling type of domination (De La Cruz 1987: 248–9).

Restructuring Reproduction

This was a crisis, we add as the point on which the greatest emphasis should be laid, in terms of both the production of goods and the reproduction of labour power; a crisis of the model of development which also concerns the way in which labour power is produced and reproduced.

On one hand, the crisis determined greater control and repression of those concerned with reproduction. On the other, it opened up space for a reform of the context in which reproduction is pursued, starting with the lifestyle and living conditions of the family nucleus, which was still considered as the basic unit of reproduction despite its great shortcomings in the Venezuelan situation (G. F. Dalla Costa, 1989a). The slant of policies for social reproduction was explicitly seen as concerning women, above all, since it is they who are principally responsible for reproduction (Ministerio de la Juventud 1985b; Ministerio de la Familia 1986).

Two aspects of these policies were clear enough in Venezuela during the 1980s. The first was a revival of repression against women in order to exert greater control over all female behaviour antagonistic, or simply unfunctional, to the current 'austerity' policy. Knowledge of the context of female criminality, in specifically penal terms, was improved (Ministerio de la Familia 1987a; Del Olmo 1987), and women's behaviour was thus more effectively fenced in. Prostitution, for example, which often represents the sole means of survival in a paralysed economy, was held up for clearer public condemnation and treated as an area of deviant female conduct that must be uprooted from the family context.

Traditionally, the osmosis between prostitution and family in Venezuela, as in many underdeveloped areas, was experienced by proletarians as more of a necessity for so many families than as the immorality of so many women (G. F. Dalla Costa 1989a). But prostitution was now persecuted by the state as behaviour detrimental to the family, to minors, and to the community. Strong tones and a wide use of the media were combined in an ideological campaign against bad mothers in whom what was previously the simple norm in the population's reproductive style was now judged as maternal irresponsibility. Leaving a minor uncared for at home to go dancing with friends on Saturday evening now became a reason for condemning a young *caribeña* mother. Should her outing result in an accident or crime, measures would be taken to declare her irresponsible and remove her children from her care.

Even if the context was different, the policy of removing minors from their parents coincided in time with a similar trend in the developed countries, where measures of this type against allegedly irresponsible parents have been more widely used than in the past, again without the provision of substantial help to improve the living conditions in which the children must be raised.

What is even clearer is that the state was experimenting with new systems of social control by legitimizing wider public intervention on the criteria and forms of reproduction (G. F. Dalla Costa 1989b). This operation above all concerned women and their responsibilities. In general terms, the widening of repression against women shows how far a rigid control of her role is believed to be strategic and crucial for the whole set-up of society, not least for maintaining an equilibrium teetering continually on the brink of crisis. This control is exercised all the more extensively over women from so-called 'marginal' social strata where, clearly, their role is particularly central to social stability.

But, during the 1980s, the second major aspect of reproduction policy came to maturation: an ample family reform and, as part of it, a reform of the relationship between the sexes. The new body of law tended to create a family configuration more similar in formal terms to families in the developed countries, since it was believed it would prove to be more functional as society's reproductive unit in future years, whatever that future might be for a country that would be moving in the more complex, more competitive and more highly qualified international context of the 1990s. The new family model was seen as potentially able to absorb, in material and ideological terms, the hammer blows that were expected to continue striking Venezuela throughout the decade since, as we have seen, it would remain an oil-dependent country.

Alongside this attempt to make the dictates of Venezuela's family law more similar to the legislation and new family codes now in force in many advanced capitalist countries, various initiatives similar to those found in some industrial nations were promoted to safeguard women against violence inside and outside the family, sexual abuse, etc. (for example, the creation of municipal safe houses for the victims of beatings or rape, with the provision of legal assistance) (Alvarez 1987; Avesa 1987; Jimenez and Acevedo 1987). In this connection, too, one should note that how the new measures were put into effect was anything but linear, because of the obstacles raised by political and social forces wanting to maintain the *status quo*. Defence against violence and reform of the family are, in fact, two areas in which women have shown an outstanding commitment to ensuring that the projects made progress.

For the labour code, too, there were vast projects for reform

(Congreso de la Republica 1985) in which women appear more clearly as the subjects of emancipatory policies (Ministerio de la Familia 1986). Once again, the legislation was similar to labour reforms in the more advanced countries. Greater attention was given to maternity leave, and greater controls were placed on the organization and working of firms using female labour (to check whether rooms were supplied for breast-feeding, care of newborn children, etc.). Above all, greater opportunities were legislated for women in access to all jobs traditionally reserved for men, in heavy industry or on night shifts, under wage conditions that were at least officially to be equal. In formal terms, these advances were certainly important. They are also significant for the insight they give into how the state was seeking to reform itself, in its handling not only of the apparatus of production, but also of expectations as to the woman's role, the latter undoubtedly envisaged as including double employment under stronger rules of social discipline.

Housework and the Devaluation of Labour Power

In substantial terms, however emancipatory they might be, the measures were simply the backdrop for a policy which required women to intensify their contribution in terms of housework. Throughout the 1980s, new stimuli were offered to achieve greater participation in this form of labour, in a context in which there was a deepening of the family's 'traditional' sexual division of labour and a clear deterioration in the material conditions under which housework was done. At the same time, the pressures were higher from both the precariousness of family subsistence and the state's new strategies of control.

In its mechanisms for reproducing labour power, the development model's historically crucial moment of crisis came at the end of the 1970s (M. Dalla Costa 1982, 1985, 1988) when, in both advanced and developing countries, there was an international convergence of women's demands for an end to the unpaid provision of the most generalized form of women's labour, housework. In other words, a rising wave of struggles linked to social reproduction detonated a crisis in the model of housework in which the labour remained unpaid. In their movements, struggles and other actions, women began to place the eradication of this model as an irreducible condition for achieving a new political bargaining power on the organization of labour, so that living and work conditions as a whole could be lifted to a higher level. Figures for the mass of unpaid housework supplied world-wide finally entered the debate, and there were condemnations of this free labour, which was identified as one of the conditions determining the weakness of the market for labour power as a whole. From the proletariat's viewpoint, the argument added, housework was an economically unrecognized area in the provision of labour power that offered a space for manoeuvre in maintaining low wages. In the last analysis, it permitted a continual devaluation of labour power.

The important aspect of state social reproduction policies in the 1980s was the attempt to breathe new life into a model of housework at the world level, in opposition to the women's rejection of it internationally. The result was an increase in work rates and a lengthening of the working day, with especially burdensome consequences for women in the underdeveloped areas. As we have seen, formally speaking, this more intense exploitation was coupled with legal reform and provisions to safeguard women. Approved in all parsimony, these were designed to channel a large part of women's energies and commitment towards specific paths of emancipation, as well as to give the state a more democratic face in the eyes of the female population (G. F. Dalla Costa 1989b).

Another and by no means secondary *leitmotif* was the important increase in the presence of women within the state. In the 1980s, numerous professional women, women functionaries and female social scientists joined various state organizations, contributing to promoting a female consensus and also in many cases contributing to more favourable policies toward women, while often censoring the debate on the woman's condition through omission, for example, by denying a hearing to the material produced and the advances made as regards attributing a wage to housework. Thus, we repeat, even if against a renewed backdrop of reform, what was quite clear, in Venezuela but also throughout Latin America, was that state policy on reproduction during the economic crisis of the 1980s rested on a strategy of reasserting housework, with the implicit aim of weakening the woman's position. At a time when the developing countries' debt took on giant proportions, the housework model was seen as optimal for the provision of women's labour because it cost nothing to governments or entrepreneurs and offered enormous potential for improving living conditions in the proletarian social strata amid widening and deepening pauperization. It could also function as a handy substitute for the essential services being slashed from the public budget.

In our view, this is how one should read the emergence of a new institutional recognition of the importance of housework. In Venezuela, notwithstanding the absence of an extensive feminist movement in the 1970s, the 1980s saw important developments in the debate on women and the family. This was accompanied by campaigns to improve housework methods – as we have noted, Venezuelan women have traditionally lacked high qualifications in housework (G. F. Dalla Costa 1989a) – to improve the basic operational unit, the family, by making it function more rationally, with greater constancy and greater continuity.

In the developing areas as a whole, reform arrived as women increasingly rejected housework, amidst a greater opening of the job market thanks to political pressure from women to achieve their own income. In Venezuela, however, the reforms were approved when women were under ever heavier pressure to produce massive quantities of housework, and in a backward form, just when the job market was worsening significantly.

In the decade of the crisis, housework was enforced again by giving it a new framework and fitting it out with a new ideology. Its uses as an aid to survival in utter poverty, as an 'adjustment' factor against hunger, and as a factor in promoting forms of solidarity in the family and the community, were enhanced through an old proposal dressed out in new colours by updating its context, not least with support for volunteer work. A sort of long-protracted failure of political recognition that represented Third World women as imprisoned by the primordial conditions of the subsistence economy (in villages, etc.) was replaced by a more up-to-date phase of the debate. Housework seemed to take on new dignity and value wherever it was effected. Yet this appreciation was not matched by economic recognition. Moreover, people were urging that housework should find wider currency in community service situations, precisely because of its effectiveness in zero-cost social reproduction. Not only in the family, then, but in the community, too, this type of labour was blasted back into orbit as a vector for promoting solidarity and volunteer work and fostering activities that can get things done without getting anything in return.

In the years of the crisis, housework took on an explicit role as one axis in the debt debate, for economists and national and international planners and officials. Its utility was obvious, while the worsening of the woman's condition was declared by one and all: *La crisis esta à los hombros de las mujeres* (the crisis is a burden on the women's shoulders).

Little light has been focused on the contradictoriness of this important connection between the intensification of housework and international indebtedness, on their role in shaping perspectives and a reality in conflict and in contradiction with the paths of emancipation proposed by the reforms. Formally speaking, housework was treated for some time as a chapter apart, in the context of the female condition, the family, or new forms of solidarity and community initiative. Its encounters with the macrocategories of the debt were less visible.

Later, though, important international bodies – the International Labour Organization, above all – and some national banks began to adopt the analysis of housework developed by the feminist debate during the 1970s, openly and point by point, particularly its contribution regarding the analysis of economic crisis. Yet they ignored that analysis's rejection of housework as unpaid labour and as a surrogate for social services. For the rest, everything was registered with precision and incorporated into the approach.

These institutions also admitted openly the delay with which they had dealt with issues of such importance for the crisis, as well as for all those social strata living in poverty or entering it. Additionally, they identified housework as a device functional to the take-off of the *politica de ajuste* – a precious device capable of combining survival with recession, the containment of poverty with the lack of a wage, and the containment of conflict without any redistribution of resources.

In some cases, these analyses reach far enough to declare quite explicitly that all approaches to poverty and welfare levels are dependent on the quantity and quality of housework supplied; that housework works as a formidable *variable de ajuste*.

> Despite the importance of the theme and, on occasions, because as we have noted the housewife's activities enjoy little social recognition, those activities have so far not been the object of systematic research in the [Latin American] region....
>
> The importance of unremunerated housework is particularly great in sectors whose monetary income, coming to a large degree from informal employment, is insufficient to acquire the basket of goods needed to satisfy fundamental needs on the market. This importance is growing and extending to other social sectors that are growing poor in a crisis such as the present one (International Labour Organization 1984: 1).

Explicitly including the profit-directed forms of labour carried out at home (production of goods for direct sale on the market, cottage industries etc.), these institutions found that such labour, which in times of crisis becomes superimposed on what is considered more strictly as housework, occupies its space and time and intensifies its work rates:

> Precisely as a consequence of the crisis, the quantitative and qualitative importance of these tasks increases. The fall in monetary income is compensated for only partially by the increase in women's participation in the market ... it determines an intensification of productive effort in the domestic nucleus to substitute for goods that were previously bought.... The recession reveals in all their amplitude housework's importance and strategic nature (International Labour Organization 1984: 4).

An attempt was also made to measure how important housework is, in the context of the crisis, for social welfare levels, and to what extent it functions as a corrective for poverty:

> economic welfare (understood as an available volume of goods and services to satisfy needs) still depends to a considerable degree on work carried out in families on the margin of market relations (International Labour Organization 1984: 15).

And again

> There are many ways of defining poverty.... Even if, obviously, an insufficiency of monetary income determines an inadequate satisfaction of basic needs, it is not a foregone conclusion that this is the only way of satisfying these needs. If that were the case, it is very probable that a large proportion of the poorest social strata who form a large part of the population in the underdeveloped countries would be unable to cope even with mere physical subsistence (International Labour Organization 1984: 16).

The circle closes with the *variables de ajuste*, whereby housework appears in all its multiple functions.

> Housework's nature as *variable de ajuste* is twofold. On one hand, there is its direct and evident role in procuring certain goods and services which, because of the insufficient monetary revenue accruing to the 'active' members of the family group, cannot be bought on the market or delegated to remunerated third persons. On the other hand, there is an indirect role which, even if less obvious, is just as important. Once unremunerated housework's compensatory nature has been defined (in the sense of an implicit contribution to family income), it consists in enabling the 'active' members to adjust the price of their labour (or in the relevant case /of cottage industries/ the entrepreneurial profit) downwards as a means for reducing in monetary terms the gap in physical productivity that separates them from formal firms, giving them a competitive capability that would otherwise be very difficult to obtain (International Labour Organization 1984: 17).

But, then, if this is the context, one can also find a vector for *de ajuste* strategies in so-called Latin American *machismo* in so far as it also functions as a channel for violent pressures to ensure that the woman works, if not for love, at least by intimidation (G. F. Dalla Costa 1978):

> despite an increase in housework as a mechanism for compensating the fall in family income, the men do not do their bit. One observation is that, in many family units where they (the men) are unemployed, they fail to help the women even though, involuntarily perhaps, they have more time of their own. As far as one can see, the crisis tends to strengthen the traditional

cultural canons, which are not prejudiced by the fact that, in the crisis, the men's function as the family's provider is weakened (International Labour Organization 1984: 5).

In this respect, it should in any case be noted that a certain concern is emerging in international bodies for housework to be divided more equally between the sexes, a concern that is probably due to the wide circulation now gained by this issue at the international level.

Mere encouragement of a more equal distribution of housework between women and men is in any case a long way from responding to the demands for a smaller workload and more welfare expressed in the women's struggles. Above all, it sidesteps the demand being advanced with increasing strength for a wholly different type of development which would open up new life possibilities for both women and men.

In a world context of increasingly relentless impoverishment – and notwithstanding the new attention to democracy between the couple now shown by some international bodies – both sexes are in fact being invited to accept the intensification of their unpaid labour. This may prove misleading with respect to a recognition of the worsening condition of Third World women, precisely in so far as international finance is seeking to compensate for its effectiveness in the creation of poverty at the planetary level through readjustment of the micro-dimensional relation lived by impoverished partners.

Bibliography

AA. VV. (1987). *Venezuela hacia el 2000. Desafíos y opciones.* Caracas: Editorial Nueva Sociedad.

Alvarez, O. (1987). *Elementos psicosociales del maltrato a la mujer: los antecedentes familiare de la pareja.* Consejo Municipal del Distrito Federal, Comisión Educación, Casa Municipal de la Mujer del Distrito federal, Convenio Ucv, V Jornadas Venezolanas de Psicologia Social, Caracas.

Anderson, L. (1987). 'Debito estero: esplosione della crisi/2'. *Il Progetto*, 7, 39 (May–June).

Avesa (1987). *Asociacion Venezolana para una educacion sexual alternativa*, Duplicated. Caracas.

Banco Central de Venezuela (BCV) (1978–86). Anuarios de Cuentas Nacionales, Caracas.

Blanco, C. (1987). *Elementos para una politica anti-inflacionaria en una estrategia economia.* Duplicated, Caracas.

Carrera Damas F. (1978). *El comportamiento sexual del venezolano, tomo 1.* Caracas: Monte Avila Ed.

Cartaya, V. (1986). *Empleo e ingresos en Venezuela: situación actual, perspectivas y alternativas.* Work in progress, Instituto Latinoamericano de Investigaciones Sociales, Caracas.

Cartaya, V. (undated). *El mercado de trabajo en Venezuela en el periodo reciente.* Caracas: Instituto Latinoamericano de Investigaciones Sociales.

Castillo, A. (undated). *La crisis y el empleo femenino en la Venezuela actual.* Duplicated, Caracas.

Castillo, A. (1985). *La crisis y la situación de la mujer trabajadora en Venezuela.* In Ministerio de la Juventud, *Trabajo femenino.* Caracas.

Centro de Estudios del Desarrollo de la Universidad Central de Venezuela (Cendes) (1983). *Elementos de la Crisis Economica Mundial y de Venezuela.* Cuadernos de Cendes, No. l. Caracas: Editorial Ateneo de Caracas.

Centro de Investigaciones en Ciencias Sociales (Cisor) (1973). *Los jovenes de Venezuela.* Examen de datos estadisticos, unpublished, Caracas.

Centro de Investigaciones en Ciencias Sociales (Cisor) (1976). *Infancia, juventud y familia, situación y evolución según datos estadisticos.* Unpublished, Caracas.

Chossudovsky, M. (1977). *La miseria en Venezuela.* Valencia: Vadell Hermanos.

Congreso de la Republica (1985). *Anteproyecto de Ley Organica del Trabajo presentado por el senador vitalicio dr. Rafael Caldera.* Caracas: Ediciones del Congreso de la Republica.

Cordiplan (1982). *Informe Social,* No. 2.

Dalla Costa, G. F. (1978). *Un lavoro d'amore.* Roma: Edizione delle donne.

Dalla Costa, G. F. (1980). *La riproduzione nel sottosviluppo. Un caso: il Venezuela.* Padova: Cleup.

Dalla Costa, G. F. (1985). 'Le politiche educative dei paesi in via di sviluppo e centralità del soggetto femminile'. In *Scuola Democratica,* 2 (April–July). Venezia: Marsilio Editori.

Dalla Costa, G. F. (1988). 'Production et reproduction au Venezuela pendant la phase de développement des années '70. Aspects des politiques sociales'. *Cahiers de l'Apre (Cnrs),* 7 (May). Paris.

Dalla Costa, G. F. (1989a). *La riproduzione nel sottosviluppo. Lavoro delle donne, famiglia e Stato nel Venezuela degli anni '70.* Milano: Angeli.

Dalla Costa, G. F. (1989b). 'Lavoro e rapporti di sesso nelle politiche degli anni '80 in Venezuela'. In A. Del Re (ed.), *Stato e rapporti sociali di sesso.* Milano: Angeli.

Dalla Costa, M. (1982). 'Percorsi femminili e politica della riproduzione della forza-lavoro negli anni '70'. In *La critica sociologica,* 61 (April–July).

Dalla Costa, M. (1985). 'Politiche del lavoro e livelli di reddito. E le donne?' In *Sociologia del lavoro in Italia e in Francia, Sociologia del Lavoro,* 26–27 (1985–6). Milano: Angeli.

Dalla Costa, M. (1988). 'Domestic labour and the feminist movement in Italy since the 1970s'. In *International Sociology,* 3, 1 (March).

De La Cruz, R. (1987). 'Alternativas frente a la declinación del modelo socio-economico actual'. In AA. VV. (1987).

Del Olmo, R. (1987). *La crisis economica y la criminalización de la mujer latino-*

americana. Duplicated, Caracas.

Despacho del ministro de estado para la participación de la mujer en el desarrollo (1979). *Principales tendencias y caracteristicas de la participación de la mujer venezolana en el proceso de desarrollo venezolano.* Caracas.

El Nacional (1987). 'Disminuir el desempleo a menos de un 9 per cent busca presupuesto '88'. Commentary on a speech delivered by the Ministro de Hacienda, Manuel Azpurna, to the Chamber of Deputies. 14 October.

Equipo Proceso Politico (1978). *CAP 5 Años. Un juicio critico.* Caracas: Editorial Ateneo de Caracas.

Faleto, E. and Martner, G. (eds) (1986). *Repensar el futuro. Estilos de desarrollo.* Caracas: Editorial Nueva Sociedad.

Fundación del niño (1976). *Memoria anual.*

Garcia, H. (1987). *Proyecto Formulacion del Plan Integral de Pobreza Critica en Venezuela (Revisión del Proyecto Estrategico de Pobreza Critica del VII Plan de la Nación).* Report of the Ministerio de la Familia, Programa de Naciones Unidas para el Desarrollo. Caracas.

Gazeta Oficial (1987). No. 33.707 (24 September) (Decree No. 1,538 of 24 April 1987). 'Bono compensatorio del salario y del gasto de transporte'. Caracas.

Haussman, R. (1987). 'Venezuela 2000: el futuro de la economia no petrolera', in AA. VV., *Venezuela hacia el 2000*, Caracas: Editorial Nueva Sociedad.

Instituto Nacional de Nutrición (undated). *El gobierno democratico combate la desnutrición.* Caracas.

International Labour Organization (ILO) (1984). *Mujeres en sus casas.* Lima: ILO Regional Office for Latin America and the Caribbean.

Izaguirre Porras, M. (1986) 'Las lecciones de la crisis (Venezuela 1983)'. In *Cuadernos del Cendes*, 5 (1986). Caracas: Vadell Hermanos Editores.

Jimenez, A. and Acevedo, C. (1987). *Caracterización socio-economica de la usuaria de la Casa Municipal de la Mujer.* Consejo Municipal del Distrito Federal, Municipio Libertador, Casa Municipal de la Mujer, Distrito Federal, Venezuela.

La Repubblica (1989). 'Il Venezuela lancia l'S.O.S.'. 4 March.

Ley General de aumento de sueldos, salarios, salario minimo, jubilación y pensiones de viejez, invalidez y muerte (1979). 2 vols.

Malavé Mata, H. (1987). *Los extravios del poder. Euforia y crisis del populismo en Venezuela.* Caracas: Universidad Central de Venezuela, Ediciones de la Biblioteca.

Martner, G. (ed.) (1986). *America Latina hacia el 2000.* Caracas: Editorial Nueva Sociedad.

Martner, G. (1987). 'La situación internacional y los desafíos para el futuro de America Latina'. In AA. VV. (1987).

Mayorca, J. M. (1977). *La criminalidad de la burguesia.* Work presented for university professorship at the Law Faculty, Universidad Central de Venezuela, Caracas.

Maza Zavala, D. F. and Malavé Mata, H. (1980). *Venezuela: dominación y disidencia 1958–1978.* Mexico: Editorial Nuestro Tiempo.

Méndez Castellano, H. (1985). *Aproximación a la salud de la Venezuela del siglo XXI*. Caracas: Cuadernos Lagoven.

Méndez Castellano, H. (1987). *Perfiles culturales, sociales y economico del venezuelano*. Caracas: Fundacredesa.

Ministerio de la Familia, Oficina Nacional de la Mujer (1986). *Propuesta de la Oficina Nacional de la Mujer del Ministerio de la Familia al proyecto de reforma de la ley del trabajo del dr. Rafael Caldera, presentadas por la ministra Virginia Olivo de Celli al Congreso Nacional el dia 6 de marzo de 1986.*

Ministerio de la Familia, Oficina Nacional de la Mujer (1987a). *Documento del taller de reforma del codigo penal concerniente a la familia y a la mujer en Venezuela*. Caracas.

Ministerio de la Familia, Dirección General de Promoción de la Mujer. (1987b). *Analisis y evaluación de los programas*. Duplicated, Caracas.

Ministerio de Justicia, Dirección de Prevención del Delito (1976). *Lineamientos y directrices nacionales de la dirección de prevención del delito para 1977, II Convención Nacional de Prevención del Delito*. November.

Ministerio de Justicia, Dirección de Prevención del Delito (1977). *Estudio monografico sobre prostitución*. Caracas.

Ministerio de la Juventud, Oficina Nacional de la Mujer (undated). *Programa defensa a la familia contra maltratos*. Caracas.

Ministerio de la Juventud, Dirección de Familia, Oficina de la Mujer (1985a). *Trabajo Femenino*. Caracas: Talleres de Impresos Altuve Hnos., C.A.

Ministerio de la Juventud, Oficina Nacional de la Mujer (1985b). *Diagnostico analitico de la situación de la mujer en Venezuela*. Caracas.

Ministerio de la Juventud (1986a). *Marco global de la politica social del estado*. Duplicated, Caracas.

Ministerio de la Juventud (1986b). *Propuesta de organización del Ministerio de la Familia*. Duplicated, Caracas.

Ministerio de la Juventud, Oficina Nacional de la Mujer (1986c). *Propuesta para un plan nacional de la mujer en el bienio '87–'88*. Caracas.

Ministerio de Sanidad y Asistencia Social (1976). *Programa de Planificación Familiar*.

Misle, G. J. F. (1987). *El estado y la politica comercial*. Duplicated, Caracas.

Oficina Central de Estadistica e Informatica (Ocei) (1979). *Encuesta nacional de fecundidad 1977*. Informe especial.

Oficina Central de Estadistica e Informatica (Ocei) (1986). *Conyuntura economica*. N. 5, IV trimestre.

Oficina Central de Estadistica e Informatica (Ocei) (1978–85). *Encuesta de Hogares por muestreo*. Caracas.

Pereira, I. (1986). *Lineamientos generales para una nueva estrategia social*. Duplicated. Caracas.

Petras, F. L. and Morley, M. H. (1983). *Petrodollars and the State: the Failure of the State Capitalist Development in Venezuela*. In Petras, J. F. *et al.*, *Capitalist and Socialist Crises in the Late Twentieth Century*. Totowa, NJ: Rowman and Allanheld Publishers.

Quintero N. E. (n. d.). *Perspectivas del mercado petrolero mundial.* Duplicated, Caracas.

Quirós Corradi, A. (1987). 'La industria petrolera. Notas para el año 2000'. In AA. VV. (1987).

Relemberg, N. S., Karner, H. and Koler, V. (1979). *Los pobres de Venezuela.* Buenos Aires: El Cid Editor.

Sela A. C. di (ed.) (1987). *Politicas de ajuste. Financiamineto del Desarrollo en America Latina.* Caracas: Editorial Nueva Sociedad.

Silva Michelena, H. (1985). 'Proceso y crisis de la economia venezolana 1960–1984'. Work presented at 'Conversatorio sobre el Desarrollo Economico del Grupo Andino', held at the Junta del Acuerdo de Cartagena, 25–27 March 1985. Duplicated, Caracas.

Silva Michelena, H. (1987). *La economia internacional y sus desafios a Venezuela.* Duplicated.

Silva Michelena, J. A. (1987). *Introducción.* In AA. VV. (1987).

Torres, G. T. (1987). *Lineamientos generales de una nueva estrategia economica para Venezuela,* duplicated, Caracas.

Valecillos, T. H. (1987). *El estado venezolano y la politica de empleo e ingresos. Principales lineamientos estrategicos,* Caracas.

Yañez Betancourt, L. (1987). *La economia venezolana: Problemas y perspectivas.* In AA. VV. (1987).

INDEX